M A

"A fascinating read! With trip... ...ous violin makers, and insight into the ...relationship between a musician and her instrument, there is much to learn and love in this book."

—Angela Correll, *Restored in Tuscany*

"A look into the mysterious world of rare violins through an endearing personal lens. A delightfully charming read that moved the music-, travel-, and history-lover in me!"

—Gabriel Lefkowitz, Concertmaster
and Resident Conductor, the Louisville Orchestra

"*Made in Italy* tells the story of an American couple's enchanting romp through Italy chasing food, wine, music—and the history of a rare, old, Cremonese violin."

—Michelle Mandro, Wine Country Women

"What a pleasure to follow the history of this remarkable violin, which is in the hands of an artist who not only appreciates its tonal qualities but also is resolute in keeping its story alive."

—Wyatt Warren, Kenneth Warren & Sons, Ltd. Violins

"Part history, part travelogue, *Made in Italy* takes you into a part of the music world you may never have thought about but will be happy to experience. Charming and thrilling, informative and action-packed, all at the same time."

—Vincenzo de Michelis, Tauck Tours

"The story of a marriage intertwined with the story of a magnificent violin. Captivating reading! Such an interesting book!"

—James Rightmyer, D.M.A.,
Fellow, the American Guild of Organists,
St. Francis in the Fields Episcopal Church

MADE IN ITALY

STRINGS ATTACHED
Four Seasons of an Italian Violin

Thomas Walter Kelley

OLD STONE PRESS

LOUISVILLE, KENTUCKY, USA

For information about special discounts for bulk purchases or autographed copies of this book, please contact John Clark, Old Stone Press at john@oldstonepress.com or the author, Thomas Walter Kelley at Cerutigb1810@gmail.com

Library of Congress Control Number: 2024902151

ISBN: 978-1-938462-66-5 (paperback)

ISBN: 978-1-938462-67-2 (eBook)

"Cheri's Violin!"
Front cover photo: Nathan Tolzmann
Back cover photo: O'Neil Arnold

Published by
Old Stone Press, an imprint of J. H. Clark & Associates, Inc

Louisville, Kentucky 40207
www.oldstonepress.com

Published in U.S.A.

MADE IN ITALY

———

STRINGS ATTACHED
Four Seasons of an Italian Violin

In memory of Charles Phillips. Fact: Without this remarkable man's guidance, mentorship, friendship, and love, Cheri would not own her Cremonese violin, I would not have had the career I enjoyed for forty years, and we would not have had this extraordinary journey to share. Our debt of gratitude is profound, and we were blessed beyond measure to have known him.

To my mom and dad, Elda and Dr. Walter Kelley, who gave me the greatest journey of all, the gift of life. They showered me with unconditional encouragement, support, and love at every step, despite my missteps. I miss them every day.

"What a difference it makes, Ebenezer, to travel the rough road of life with the right female to help bear the burden."

—Old Fezziwig, *A Christmas Carol*, by Charles Dickens

To the love of my life, Cheri, who has helped smooth out life's rough road, turning it into the most wonderfully fulfilling journey. Thank you for always believing in me and encouraging me. God brought you into my life for a reason, and what a privilege it has been to travel through life with you.

To Ethan, a joyful and gentle soul who has made our lives complete.

In memory of Shannon Marie Kelley Johnson, my oldest sister, whose enthusiasm for this book gave me so much pleasure. "I want to be the first one in line to get an autographed copy," she would say with such joy in her voice. Tragically, she passed away unexpectedly and much too soon, on August 6, 2023.

Shann, you are missed and loved more than you can imagine!

CONTENTS

SEASON II
Coming to America

SEASON III
Into the Abyss

SEASON IV
A Cremonese Legacy Secured

PROLOGUE
The Dream Becomes Reality

———

W E'VE DONE IT! We've actually done it! With the stroke of a pen, Cheri signs the bill of sale, we hand over the check, shake hands with the executive director of the Louisville Orchestra, and the sale is complete. It is ours.

After nineteen years, our dream of owning "it" is finally realized. On a hot, sunny afternoon in May 2000, in a small conference room in downtown Louisville, it is miraculously ours.

Cheri and I have just made the second-largest investment in our married life. I deliberately use the word *investment* as opposed to *purchase* because this is so much more than just an outlay of cash. Only the home we built two years earlier in 1998 is more expensive than "it"—at least, for now. However, the potential of this new investment far exceeds that of any home.

The "it" we have just purchased is a violin. Not just an ordinary, commonplace violin, but an eighteenth-century, Cremonese Italian violin with all the charisma, aura, and romance that accompanies such an instrument.

Peering into the heart of the violin through the f-hole, we can barely make out the label covered with more than two hundred years of dust and dirt. The label—written in Latin as was the custom of the day—attributes the violin to *Laurentius Guadagnini, Pater/& alumnus Antonj Straduarj/fecit Piacentie Anno 1743* (Lorenzo Guadagnini, Father /& student of Antonio Stradivari made in the year of 1743).

Cheri has played this violin, generously on loan to her from the Louisville Orchestra, for the past nineteen years, during which time, as Shakespeare might have said, "It has grappled itself to her soul." Its pedigree is impressive and much sought after. It comes replete with history from both the Old World and the New World.

Cheri at Kenneth Warren & Sons. Chicago

Weighing in at just under one pound without a chinrest (fourteen-plus ounces, to be more accurate), this lighter-than-air work of art is an acoustical marvel.

The date and city of its making are also of immense importance because violins made during the Golden Age of violin making in Cremona, Italy, include the most celebrated, coveted, and expensive names in the history of violin making: Amati, Stradivari, Guarneri, Guadagnini, and others.

As we leave our meeting, the full weight of what has just happened washes over us. Given the exorbitant cost of these instruments and the insatiable demand for them, it's still inconceivable that we now have the privilege of owning one.

In our souls, however, we both understand a fundamental truth: You never truly own one of these violins, you simply pass through its life.

A Word About the Structure of This Book

I CONFESS I'M A rules follower. I always have been, and given my age, I probably always will be. So, it should come as no surprise that when I began seriously thinking about writing this book, I envisioned it in a conventional format using conventional chapters.

However, using a conventional format quickly proved to be problematic, fraught with headaches. This is the story of the life of a fine, old, Italian violin, and our discovery of its history proved to be both intimate and circuitous. So, in keeping, I have created my own format that's also intimate and circuitous.

As I set out to create this format, the Baroque composer/violinist Antonio Vivaldi kept coming to mind. It wasn't long before I understood why. Arguably, Vivaldi's most famous work is *Le quattro stagioni (The Four Seasons)*. The more I thought about the concept of structure and Vivaldi's *Four Seasons*, the more alluring it became to convey our story not in chapters but in seasons. And so, in a reverential nod to Vivaldi's genius, I embraced the concept of using seasons rather than chapters.

One last word about structure. Vivaldi's *Le quattro stagioni* is composed of four violin concertos describing the four seasons of the year, Spring, Summer, Autumn, and Winter. However, my use of the four seasons is slightly different. While both works speak to the passage of time, Vivaldi's *Four Seasons* takes you on a journey through a calendar year. The four seasons I have envisioned relate to the seasons of our violin's life over two centuries.

Season I describes what little we know of its life in Italy. I use history and my imagination to create plausible scenarios of what might have happened to it prior to coming to America. Season II picks up the violin's journey once it arrives in America. Season III delves into an identity crisis suffered by both the violin and us. Finally, Season IV describes our elation at discovering the legacy of this beautiful Cremonese instrument. These four seasons span a time frame beginning with the birth of our violin to the present.

A Word About "Author's Whim"

I ASK MYSELF, "WHAT exactly is a whim?" The derivation of the word comes from an early sixteenth-century noun known as *whim-wham*. Our word *whim* is simply a shortened version of *whim-wham*.

In the sixteenth century, a *whim* referred to an ornamental object or trinket, a small jewel.

"That's it!" I thought. The notion of a small jewel perfectly captured the concept I had envisioned for each of the whims included at the end of each of the four seasons.

I encourage you to think of each whim as a small jewel. Each of these gems will give you another insight into the various experiences we've enjoyed throughout our journey. Some are poignant, profound even, and one offers a life lesson.

While these small jewels have nothing directly to do with our purchase of this beautiful Cremonese violin, they have everything to do with our love of Italy, its people, its cuisine, its wine, and its history. In our minds, it's virtually impossible to separate the two. Had it not been for the violin, none of this discovery would have happened.

So these small jewels are moments we will savor for the rest of our lives. As you move from season to season, it is my hope that they will also provide you with an appreciation for the place, time, joy, passion, and friendships we've developed along the way.

AUTHOR'S DISCLOSURE
Lessons in Rare Cremonese Violins

———

A DIFFICULT LIFE LESSON comes on the day you realize that things are not always as they seem. This reality is especially true in the world of fine, rare Italian violins. As we would discover even before we bought the violin, in addition to all its wonders, romance, and mystique we found a sordid world fraught with fakes, frauds, and forgeries. *Caveat emptor*—buyer beware. Enter at your own risk, even if you're a professional.

As Cheri and I began our journey, we quickly learned that our violin was not immune to this problem. So, to best understand our journey with the least amount of confusion, I feel it would be helpful for you to know upfront that our violin was not made by the person the label said it was. The label had been forged. Lorenzo Guadagnini did not make the violin. It was made by another Italian maker of historical importance, Giovanni Battista Ceruti, circa 1810, not circa 1743. That forgery would prove to have ramifications for us.

As an aside, when pronouncing Ceruti's last name, think of the word *cello*. Use that same *ch* sound, add the following, *che-ROO-tee,* and you've got it.

This is our remarkable journey through more than four decades of falling in love with this magnificent instrument, of being recipients of the greatest kindness humanity has to offer, of being thrown headlong into the quagmire of the world of fine Italian violins—and ultimately discovering what an important role this violin and its creator played as the Golden Age of violin making in Cremona came to an end.

So, pour yourself a glass of wine (Italian preferably), settle into a comfortable chair, and relax as our Ceruti takes you on our extraordinary, true, life-changing journey.

SEASON I

Early Life in Italy

———

Mia Visione (My Vision)

――――

I MAGINATION IS ONE of the most potent and creative forces we humans are blessed to have at our disposal. Thank goodness for my imagination, because without it, Season I would be devoid of anything meaningful or interesting. The reason is simple. Season I of the Ceruti's life in Italy is devoid of any facts or history. *Niente!* (Nothing!)

As is true of the plight of so many Italian violins made in the sixteenth, seventeenth, and eighteenth centuries, we know virtually nothing about their early lives. Very rarely does a violin have a paper trail to follow. For example, did the Ceruti spend all of its years in Italy in the town where it was "born," Cremona? If not, to what other towns did its journey take it? Also, how did it travel from Italy to the United States?

The answers to these questions and countless others are completely unknown. Those details seem destined to be forever shrouded in mystery.

Even in the face of that challenge, however, we do know a great deal about the era of the great Italian violin masters. And while I am neither a historian nor a professional violinist, I have had a lifelong passion for these Cremonese instruments. In addition, over the last twenty years, I have also used every opportunity to travel to Italy with Cheri to enhance my knowledge.

So, given this reality and to fill this factual void, I busied my imagination to draw upon that knowledge and experience to create hypothetical scenarios that this instrument could have experienced during that period, and that many fine Italian instruments actually did.

Even more important, by using my imagination to envision Season I, Cheri and I stumbled upon truths and facts about this instrument and its maker that we would not—could not—have otherwise known.

I call these imaginings *mia visione* (my vision). In the Italian, it is pronounced *me-ah viz-ee-oh-nay*.

The sole purpose of *mia visione* in Season I is to weave a credible story describing the life our violin might have experienced while living in Italy.

The Golden Age and the Cremonese Charisma

CHERI'S VIOLIN WAS made—well, actually, we prefer to think of it as being "born"—during what was unquestionably the most creative period in the history of violin making, and certainly one of the most creative periods in all of Western civilization.

It's impossible to overstate this period's importance, which would come to be known as the Golden Age of violin making. Something innovative and exciting was happening—a phenomenon in the enhanced shape and sound of the violin was coming into its own.

We first see this new development taking hold, gaining in popularity and demand, during the latter years of the Renaissance. It comes to life in the late sixteenth and early seventeenth centuries in the small provincial town of Cremona in the Lombardy region of Italy.

Cremona...the name itself is now synonymous with violin making—the very pinnacle of violin making. It is a sacred place, hallowed ground for violinists, string players, and *luthiers* (violin makers). Whether it be performers or *luthiers*, in the world of fine and rare Italian violins, the name *Cremona* has a spiritual, reverential quality about it.

In fact, Cremona has been christened *la Città dei violini* (the City of Violins). During the 1600s, Cremona would become the unrivaled violin-making capital of the world—the heart. It would continue to dominate the world of violin making for approximately the next hundred years. By the mid-1800s, at least in the small provincial town of Cremona, the Golden Age of violin making would come to a close.

I often wonder, what is it about Cremonese violins—the Cremonese charisma—that makes them so unique and desirable? How is it that the finest Cremonese instruments made by the finest Cremonese makers are capable of producing so many magical moments: breath-taking pyrotechnics one moment, only to be followed by the most intimate, exquisite, and haunting moments the next—those moments when a sudden gasp of air quietly catches in the back of your throat at the same time your emotions well up and the tears begin to flow, perhaps conjuring up a memory of a time and place long ago.

Part of the answer lies in their shape as perfected by the early Cremonese masters. While these instruments are beautiful and elegant, to be sure, make no mistake that, over the centuries, every curve and aspect of the instrument's design has been studied and influenced by science and acoustics.

This is essential to understand because a violin's appearance can be deceptive. It is capable of misleading the beholder into believing that, with its elegant curves, beautiful purfling, amber-brown varnish, high arching top, and back plates, it's somewhat fragile—flimsy even. But nothing could be further from the truth.

In reality, these instruments are two hundred- to three-hundred-year-old workhorses subjected to tremendous stress and pressure every day. After all, they have been exposed to all that hundreds of years of life, performing, and traveling can throw at them. And yet, in Cheri's case, just as in so many others, her violin goes to work with her every day and endures arduous, demanding workouts.

As I sit in my study on the second floor of our home, I'm privileged to have a front-row seat as, from her practice studio on the first floor, she plays Bach's Sonatas and Partitas for Unaccompanied Violin, Ysaye's "Ballade," Ravel's *Tzigane*, Cyril Scott's *Lotus Land*, and Heifetz's showpiece arrangements, to name just a fraction of her repertoire. These are ferociously demanding pieces for a violinist and equally demanding for the violin. And by the way, this doesn't begin to include the orchestral and chamber music repertoire she has played over the years.

Yet, hold one of these masterpieces in your hands and it's as if you are holding little more than a puff of air.

I rarely have the opportunity to hold the violin these days, primarily for two reasons. First, it makes Cheri very nervous, and second, since I haven't played the violin in over forty years, my satisfaction comes from admiring its beauty and craftsmanship, not from holding it. However, on those rare occasions when I do have it securely in my grasp, I still marvel at how little it weighs.

You begin to understand the physics of a violin if you think of standing in front of a loudspeaker. Visualize placing your fingers on the cone of the loudspeaker. As the music plays, you can feel the speaker's vibrations pulsate through your fingertips.

Now, visualize a violin and a bow. When a bow is drawn across the strings, the strings vibrate just like a loudspeaker, as do the top and back plates, which in turn produce most of the sound. The bridge also acts as a conduit, enabling the vibrations and sound to be transferred from the strings through the bridge into the body of the instrument.

But an even more significant miracle can be found inside the violin. It's here that you will find its heart and soul.

Running along the inside of the top piece of the instrument is the bass bar. In a nutshell, this piece of wood has been glued in place, and its purpose is to both reinforce the top of the instrument while also allowing sound and vibrations to be transferred throughout the top plate. Yet this is still not the violin's heart and soul.

Without question, the most crucial piece inside the instrument is its sound post, a simple dowel made of wood scarcely as large as most people's little finger. But make no mistake, the sound post is the heart and soul of the violin.

Its purpose is to transfer vibrations between the top and bottom plates of the instrument. And as you would expect, there is an art to placing the sound post in that precise spot that will enable the violin to produce the very best sound it can give. Move it just a millimeter one way or the other, and the sound changes completely, usually for the worse. As the violin is played, the sound post can naturally shift. As a result, periodic adjustments are required to return it to its optimal position.

The exact location that's best for each instrument is unique. Finding that sweet spot is as much art as it is science, since violins, especially fine Italian violins, can be finicky. Supposedly, the great nineteenth-century violinist and composer Nicolo Paganini was so meticulous about the placement of the sound post in his legendary Guarneri del Gesu that he took a pen and marked the precise spot that he felt resulted in the perfect sound. Because of the enormous, gorgeous, deep sound it produced, Paganini himself nicknamed his del Gesu *il Cannone*—the Cannon.

This is why violinists are so fanatical about making certain their sound post is perfectly placed. They want to ensure they can draw out every last ounce of sound the instrument has to give.

Consider also, these instruments were made hundreds of years ago—certainly before today's concert halls were conceived. None of the Cremonese makers could have visualized concert halls as we know them today.

To my mind, this is fascinating because these violins are now played in modern concert halls that can seat thousands of people. Keep in mind, these violins don't use amplification of any sort to project their sound. It's purely the instrument's power versus the hall's size and acoustics. Yet these acoustical wonders effortlessly project their sound over a symphony orchestra to the back of a hall. Soloists often say they "play to the back of the hall." And these great Cremonese violins deliver, their voice soaring over an orchestra. This is the miracle of the violin—a marvel of physics and acoustics.

Herein lies another secret of why violinists are so obsessed with their instruments. While it may seem counter-intuitive, the main reason has little to do with the physical features of their instrument, beautiful as they may be. It's what the instrument produces from within, from its heart and soul, that matters. This is why Cheri prefers to think of her violin as having been born. It has a soul.

The significance of all this takes on an entirely new meaning if you imagine you're a violinist. Envision you've played several violins over time, but you've never found the one that perfectly expresses your inner musical voice, that gives you a sense of oneness with the violin. You have yet to find that one instrument that fits you perfectly, both physically and acoustically. Sadly, many violinists never find that instrument—or worse yet, can't afford it when they do.

Now imagine picking up a violin one day and playing it long enough to discover it's as if a set of your vocal cords had been transplanted into the instrument. Imagine further that those vocal cords impeccably emulate and produce your concept of sound. Only when you find such an instrument can you truly appreciate how anyone becomes so infatuated.

This conversation takes place at all levels of the violin industry. As an example, an ongoing, light-hearted argument among violinists is whether they consider themselves a "Strad" person or a "Guarneri" person. The basis of the question is whether the violinist prefers the sound production made by a Stradivari or that of a Guarneri del Gesu because they are very different indeed. In many ways, it's a ridiculous argument because it involves such personal tastes. And besides, as Teddy Roosevelt so appropriately said, "Comparison is the thief of joy."

Imagine, for example, overhearing this conversation: "Congratulations. You're a very fortunate individual because we have a Guarneri del Gesu purchased by a private investor that is being given to you for your exclusive use for the rest of your life." Can you imagine the next words you hear out of the recipient's mouth being, "Oh, no thanks. You see, I'm a Strad person." I think not! No sane person would turn down such an offer, regardless of preference.

But people still enjoy hearing the back-and-forth bantering as to which maker, in their opinion, is superior. The famous violinist Itzhak Perlman said that he always enjoys playing a Guarneri del Gesu, that it's always a "pleasant experience." But when he picks up his Strad, he melts from the sound. The voice it creates is perfection to his ear and his soul. It's his voice. "Oh my God," is his response as he rolls his eyes. He still can't believe that his Strad produces the sounds that it does. With a mischievous smile on his face, he says that comparing a Strad person to a Guarneri person is similar to pitting Bordeaux lovers against Burgundy lovers. Both are excellent wines, but some people prefer one over the other—it's that simple.

As for comparing the men Stradivari and Guarneri del Gesu, you could not find two more opposite personalities. To say the two were even remotely similar in personality, work ethic, or their finished products would be equivalent to saying that Microsoft and Apple are identical. After all, they both make computers, right?

It is true that Stradivari and del Gesu both created violins, but that is where any similarities end.

Unlike violins today, some of which are mass-produced by machines, these violins were made by hand. Being made by hand meant that all the Cremonese makers spent countless hours imbuing life and a soul into each instrument. No two are alike.

It is usually ill-advised to generalize. However, as a rule, the violins made by Stradivari tend to have a brighter, sweeter sound, whereas those made by Guarneri del Gesu tend to have a deeper, darker voice. Of course, you can find exceptions, but as a rule, such is the case. The reality is, the best makers could create instruments that produced the concept of what they thought the sound of a violin should be, and history has shown us that their concept of sound was magic! If you're ever able to listen to a Stradivari being played immediately followed by a Guarneri del Gesu, you'll hear the difference instantly. The comparison will astound you.

For those fortunate enough to attend concerts given by world-class orchestras, a smattering of these great orchestras own a few of these Cremonese masterpieces. The Vienna Philharmonic's string section, for example, is known the world over for its legendary string sound. It owns four Stradivari violins, allowing select members to play them. The quality of these four violins adds to that sound.

So then, these violins are, without question, more than just lifeless, disembodied slabs of wood a little more than one inch thick at the beginning of their life and made a few hundred years ago. They are a means by which we humans express ourselves in a language like no other: music.

Many believe the violin's sound is the closest instrument to the human voice. In the hands of a gifted artist, sounds are produced that so closely mimic the human voice as to be astonishing.

In the spirit of full disclosure, the debate over whether Cheri is a Strad person or a Guarneri person has never seriously taken place in our home for one obvious reason: The $5 million to $20 million and higher price tags are a bit out of our reach! However, we have discussed at length the issue of the Ceruti being her voice. This issue was settled emphatically, once and for all, years ago.

We had already purchased the violin and were in Philadelphia to have the world-renowned violin shop of William Moennig & Son reappraise it for insurance purposes and to have some repair work done.

As an aside, if you ever seriously consider purchasing a fine and rare Italian violin, you should know that it can be very temperamental and expensive to maintain. Changes in geography, weather, and humidity all play a role in making them as persnickety as they are.

Since we were going to be at William Moennig & Son for at least two days while they completed their work, Dick Donovan, a longtime employee of Moennig's and an expert in restoration and repair, chose three violins from their inventory for Cheri to play. The elegant studio was located on the second floor. This gesture was much more than just the extending of professional courtesy. This was and still is common practice for the simple but critical reason that these instruments need to be played, and played regularly.

How important is it that they be played regularly? Visit the magnificent violin museum located in City Hall in Cremona, and you'll discover that while the beautiful Stradivari, Guarneri del Gesu, and Amati instruments spend much of their time on display, they are also played regularly. They are living organisms that must be played to ensure that, like a muscle, they don't atrophy.

The now-retired Andrea Mosconi was the guardian of the City Hall's violin museum for many, many years. He was responsible for playing these instruments every day for six minutes each. Again, violins are much like muscles; if not played regularly, their sound becomes tight. These instruments are organic, vibrating machines—the more they're played, the more their sound improves as the violin unleashes its full capabilities.

Moennig was always delighted to have violinists play the instruments they had in inventory. I remember this day as clearly as if it happened yesterday. Cheri picked up the first of the three violins lying on a table in front of her: a gorgeous Amati, made in the seventeenth century. It had all the classic traits of a Cremonese violin—the physical characteristics and that beautiful golden-brown varnish.

As she began playing, she took her time to allow the Amati to introduce itself to her and for her to get to know it. Before long, however, the room was filled with its glorious sound. They quickly became good friends. After a few scales, her nimble fingers played Bach, Ravel's *Tzigane,* and Mozart concerti. It all seemed so effortless to her. She was taken by the ease with which it played and its exquisite sound.

She was clearly enjoying the moment, so after a bit, I casually asked her if she would be interested in buying it—although the price tag was $600,000. She turned to me and emphatically said, "No! The Ceruti is my voice, and no other violin can replace that!"

As Mark Twain so aptly said, "There's nothing more to be learned from the second kick of a mule." So, wisely, I decided not to assert my offer a second time. I ceded the floor to her and quietly returned to my chair, realizing that this issue was settled once and for all. But I also had a renewed appreciation of the relationship between conceptualization and physical sound.

How do you explain such a relationship? It's organic. It wells up from within, from the soul. Cheri has always been clear about this. "Playing this violin is how I convey the concept of sound I hear in my mind," she says. "I first hear the sound in my mind, I then translate that sound through my fingers, and ultimately the violin gives voice to that sound." For Cheri, the Ceruti was and will always be her voice. Lesson learned.

Power Families of the Golden Age

——————

ANDREA AMATI (1505–1577) was the first violin-making superstar of the Golden Age. He not only ushered in this critical period, but his contribution was of such importance that he became known as the father of the modern violin. His creative genius ultimately designed and standardized the form, materials, and construction techniques used to make the violin as we know it. While there have been experiments and variations on the basic form that Amati created, the overall shape and size of the violin has not changed to this day.

Andrea Amati was also the father of the first family dynasty to make a name for itself in Cremona, *Casa Amati* (House of Amati). Several such family dynasties would follow throughout the Golden Age, but the *famiglia Amati* was the first.

As if to drive this point home, Andrea's grandson Niccolò would catapult the violin's status to greatness by the late 1600s. Italian violins made during this period have several unmistakable characteristics: a more robust sound, a golden, amber-brown varnish, and high-arching top and bottom plates. All these traits have become coveted hallmarks of this period.

But with the Amati family, Cremona was just beginning to etch its place in history. The city still had so much more to give. Niccolò Amati would receive additional notoriety, which would further cement his place in history. It is believed that Antonio Stradivari may have studied with him early in Stradivari's career.

As this new era evolved, improvements were made to the

sounds these wonders of physics could produce. While this remarkable period would see several brilliant violin makers create exquisite masterpieces, it would culminate with the work of two geniuses recognized to this day as the best of the best, Antonio Stradivari and Giuseppe Guarneri del Gesu (literally "of Jesus").

A brief but fascinating word about Guarneri's nickname, "del Gesu." Guarneri del Gesu had a unique way of signing the labels he placed inside his violins. He meticulously placed a cross fleury on each label and then, directly beneath it, added the Greek letters *IHS*, a direct Christian reference to the name of Jesus Christ—literally, "Jesus. Savior of men."

Stradivari and Guarneri del Gesu are the two geniuses who would take what the Amatis created and hone it to perfection. To this day, no violin rivals those made by Stradivari and Guarneri del Gesu—they are the gold standard. They are coveted and command millions of dollars.

People have wondered for centuries what makes a Stradivari or a Guarneri del Gesu so unique. Why is the competition to play one, own one, or invest in one so intense? That has been a subject of endless speculation. Some experts say in the case of Stradivari, it was the "secret varnish" he used—some kind of special alchemy. Interestingly enough, just before his death, Stradivari destroyed all his varnish recipes, so we probably won't be solving that mystery any time soon. He intentionally took his varnish secrets to the grave.

Others speculate that these instruments are great because they came from the exceptional trees of the Paneveggio forest, located in the Dolomites in Northern Italy. In fact, the Paneveggio forest has been nicknamed "The Violins' Forest." Stradivari would take long walks there. He would occasionally stop and put his ear against a tree trunk while "thumping" on it. Hearing the sound of the tree helped him determine whether it had the qualities he was seeking to create a great instrument. Interestingly, one percent of the trees in this unique forest ended up as Cremonense instruments.

Still others say it was the "mini-ice age" that occurred in Europe during this time that created the exceptional wood that produced the instruments' beautiful tone.

To all of this, I say, "Bewildering perhaps." But then again, it may simply be that genius is genius, just as with Mozart and music and Shakespeare and literature. World-renowned violin expert John Becker of John Becker and Company in Chicago perhaps said it best when asked what the secret of these violin makers was. His reply was, "They were just better than everyone else. That's the secret."

When people find out that Cheri is a professional violinist, it's not uncommon for them to ask, "Do you play a Stradivarius?" As if we had walked into the corner music shop and bought one off the rack!

Notice the name *Stradivarius* is in the Latin form of his surname—*Stradivari* is Italian. We've often thought how fun it would be for her to answer, "Why yes. Yes, I do!" But that's not the case. The reality is that while Stradivari made about 1,100 instruments, only about 600 survive to this day. They are rare and often cost several million dollars. The greater the violin's pedigree and history, the higher the price.

As unfair and egregious as this may seem, most violinists are in no financial position to be able to afford such instruments, at least not solely on a musician's income. A much more common practice is for a private investor or syndicate of investors to loan these violins to deserving recipients. Thank goodness for these benefactors. Because of their generosity, deserving violinists have the opportunity to perform on these amazing Golden Age instruments.

And so it was into this glorious era that Cheri's violin was born.

Our First Visit to Venice

THIS FINE, OLD, Italian violin came into our lives in 1980. Naturally, we were curious about its history. Where had it been? What kind of life had it lived? We could not have known at the time the extraordinary journey we would take answering these questions: the countless people who would help us, the international travel, and the lifelong friendships we'd form along the way.

But it wasn't until we visited Venice in June 2003 that *mia visione*—my vision of its early life—began to form.

Venice has been romantically nicknamed "la Serenissima" ("the Most Serene"). I love that name; I love saying that name. It's calming and pleasurable at the same time. Like so many Italian words, it gently rolls off the tongue and is soothing to the ears when you place just the slightest emphasis on the second syllable— *la Sere-NEEE-ssima*. It evokes the most marvelous images in my mind. Venice truly is a magical city, a city that grabs your senses by the lapels, waking them up and engaging them to their full extent.

While we were wandering in and out of the numerous passageways and over the equally numerous bridges, Cheri stopped me, took me by the arm, and said, "Do you realize this isn't Disney World? This is real. It's not plastic. Real people built it, defended it, ruled it, and made their lives here. Just like they do today." That is a fact, and the profound point she was making resonated deep within me.

I have never much cared for fitting into a demographic or stereotype, but there was no way to avoid it here. The truth is, we were typical tourists, eyes wide open in awe of what we were seeing, mouths slightly agape, completely overwhelmed by the beauty of the city.

One museum in particular proved to us that fine old Cremonese violins did, in fact, play an integral role in the musical life of Venice. It was a museum featuring old stringed instruments. We took our time stopping and admiring each instrument along the way. While meandering, we came across several violins made by prestigious makers. And while these violins may have been born in Cremona, they had clearly lived in Venice as well. One was a beautiful violin made by Giovanni Battista Ceruti in 1810. Perhaps Cheri's Ceruti also had made the relatively short journey from Cremona to Venice during its life in Italy.

This was an exciting possibility, and thus *mia visione* began to form.

A Canal-Side Dinner

O N ONE LOVELY Venetian evening, we dined at Ristorante da Raffaele—a charming canal-side ristorante on a popular gondolier route. As we entered, I announced in the best Italian I could muster, *"Ho una prenotazione per due"* ("I have a reservation for two"). We were quickly escorted to a table overlooking the canal.

It was covered in pink linens with one lit candle in the center and a vase holding a solitary rose. Draped over the wrought-iron railing next to us were flower boxes bursting with beautiful purple flowers. Without a doubt, this evening was going to be *perfetto* (perfect).

As the evening progressed, and much to our great pleasure, several gondolas drifted by while serenading us with the most enchanting *armonica* (accordion) music. When you engage a gondolier, you have the option of paying additional euros for the added entertainment of an accordion player or even an Italian tenor. We remember one couple that had spent lavishly on their romantic gondola adventure. Not only had they hired an accordion player but the Italian tenor as well.

The tenor was an older, charismatic gentleman with a robust voice who stood proudly at the front of the gondola, gesticulating with his hands while he sang. As the gondola quietly glided by, and with his lungs filled to capacity, he sang "O solo mio" to this couple—and the rest of us—with all his heart! And while his marvelous voice was still strong, in truth it was a bit past its prime.

His vibrato was more like a wide warble, which only made it more endearing. The twinkle in his eye and his natural flair made it clear that he knew he had all of us in the palm of his hand.

We were utterly enchanted as the music reverberated off the bricks and stones of the centuries-old buildings lining the canal. *Magia* (magic)!

Well, who could resist the intoxicating charm of such a setting? Our dinner was complete, but not wanting to let this evening slip away, a gondola ride was meant to be. So I negotiated a price with an enthusiastic gondolier, and Cheri and I savored what remained of this special day while enjoying a quiet and very romantic Gondola ride—*senza* (without) the accordion or the tenor.

Return to Venice

WE RETURNED TO Venice in October 2011, but this visit would be vastly different from our first. This time, we were on a mission, a quest that would prove to be a forerunner of possibilities. This visit would breathe life into *mia visione* by showing us what our Ceruti may have experienced during its "adolescent years" in Venice.

Flying into Venice's Marco Polo airport is something you really should experience. As your aircraft makes its final, lumbering approach toward the runway, you have marvelous views of the *città* (city) as you peer out the tiny window of your aircraft. Because Venice is relatively compact, you can easily see it spread out before you, including many of the surrounding islands. All of it, naturally, is bound by water—lots and lots of water.

As you continue your descent, you become ever more aware of the water below getting closer and closer until suddenly the runway seems to appear out of nowhere, leaping up to meet you. And just that quickly, you've landed in Venice.

After taxiing to our gate, we got off the plane and made our way to the baggage carousel to claim our luggage. Getting from the airport to our hotel was another unexpected adventure. When you've been traveling for hours, you're tired, a bit cranky, and unexpected experiences aren't always high on your list. But that was not the case here. What we were about to experience became memorable.

With our luggage in tow, we made the short walk from the

terminal to the piers, where we planned to catch the *vaporetto* (waterbus) from the airport to our hotel. But no sooner had we gotten to the piers than we discovered that the workers had gone on strike—just for one day. We looked at each other and said, "Great. Now what? Of all the days, why did they have to strike today?" With no advanced warning, there we were, stranded, or so it seemed.

It was only then that we noticed that next to the *vaporetto* piers were several sleek, much faster, and, yes, more expensive water taxis. We realized we were in luck. We hired one with no more effort than it would take to hail a cab on Fifth Avenue in New York. And thankfully, we did it before the throngs of travelers behind us discovered that getting from the airport to Venice was going to take a lot of work.

This adventure was quickly turning into a fantastic quasi-James Bond experience. In no time, our captain had loaded our luggage, and we were whisked away in a streamlined, aerodynamic water taxi. All there was to do now was to sit back and relax.

I took great comfort, twisted as though it may seem, as I watched the *vaporetto* piers disappear into the distance behind our wake. We were so relieved to be out of that mess.

So we simply sat back and basked in the exhilarating ride to our hotel. We agreed we couldn't have had a greater welcome to Venice than to see a sun-drenched, crystal-clear blue sky above the shimmering Adriatic Sea.

We careened past what seemed like endless pilings lining our route into Venice, but in about forty-five minutes, we arrived at the piers in front of the Londra Palace, our hotel, located at the mouth of the Grand Canal. Having stayed here during our first visit, we were familiar with the hotel and its surroundings. We wheeled our luggage into the lobby. With typical Italian efficiency, the front desk checked us into our suite, where we collapsed from exhaustion.

I admit to having an annoying habit when traveling. I want to begin sightseeing as soon as we get to our hotel. I find it virtually impossible to turn off the adrenaline. I am revved up and anxious to go.

However, on this particular day, Cheri was in no mood to walk down to the hotel lobby, let alone walk around Venice. She was worn out. And so it went back and forth: "I think we should go." "But I'm too tired." "I know, but I want to get going." "I just need to rest for a while, then we'll go."

I kept pushing (I like to think of it more as encouragement). She finally relented, probably more to shut me up as opposed to me having changed her mind. Regardless, she set out with me. This was a calculated risk on my part—but a calculated risk that paid off.

Every so often, you uncover a gem during your travels. It's as if the stars align and at that particular moment in time and in that particular place, you're graced with an experience that becomes a favorite lifelong memory.

Such was the case as we crossed over a small bridge spanning one of the many canals and stumbled upon the delightful Vino Vino Osteria Enoteca. It was tucked under an archway next to one of Venice's many bridges and gondolier routes. The osteria was cozy and inviting; it seemed to say, "Come inside; savor the moment." We walked in, chose a comfortable table, and settled in while admiring such unique, homey touches as the lace-covered lights hanging from the heavy wood beams. We both let out a sigh and agreed, it felt so good to sit and give our legs a rest.

Well, as cozy and inviting as the exterior might have been, the reception we received inside from the wait staff was anything but inviting. It was clear they were used to dealing with an ill-mannered clientele who wanted little more than a quick bite to eat. Our service was curt and abrupt. Getting the customer in and out seemed to be their only mission.

But as is so often true in life, you get out of an experience what you put into it.

Cheri and I began to realize that my inadequate Italian could work in our favor. I have several Italian phrases memorized that I can use to get by when needed. But please be clear, I am not now, nor will I ever be, fluent in Italian. And besides, Italians have the most irritating habit of answering my questions in Italian when I ask them in Italian. I'm instantly at a loss.

Nevertheless, I was grateful at that moment because it forced us to begin asking our server questions about the menu. *"Scuzi. Can you tell me what is formaggio stagionato?* I see. And what about the *formaggio misto?"*

These questions opened a dialogue, which sent a subtle message to him that we were here for an experience. We weren't hoping to rush through our *pranzo* (lunch) just so we could move on to the next sight to check off our list. This was a moment meant to be savored.

It should not be forgotten that Cheri was still somewhat put out with me for dragging her along on our walking tour. As if that wasn't bad enough, when you're already exhausted, the last thing you want is to have to put up with attitude from a rude server.

Clearly, I was in a precarious position that could tilt either way. Until that is, our server asked one question, one glorious, magical question: *"Vuoi ordinare un bicchiere di vino?"* ("Would you like to order a glass of wine?")

That one simple question turned our lunch from an irritating, forgettable experience to one of Cheri's fondest memories from all our Italian adventures. And so, while we waited for our meal, she ordered a glass of Barolo, and I ordered a glass of Brunello. It wasn't long before our server placed a glass of ruby-red Barolo in front of her. I raised my glass of Brunello and we toasted each other: *"Buon appetito."* As soon as she took her first sip, she visibly relaxed. I could see the tension drain out of her.

As you might expect, during our Italian adventures, we've enjoyed many wines over the years, including some exquisite Barolos. But for some reason, at that moment, in that place, she couldn't recall the last time she had tasted one that she enjoyed as much. She relished every drop.

Venice can have this effect on you. When our server saw her reaction, the point was finally driven home that we were here to cherish this experience and Vino Vino's cuisine.

From that moment on, our waiter took marvelous care of us. Being in this place with Cheri was *Paradiso!* (Heaven!)

An Evening with Vivaldi

As you wander around Venice, it's impossible not to be barraged with vendors hawking tickets to all sorts of concerts. We usually go out of our way to avoid them. Having traveled in Europe for many years, Cheri and I have discovered that when it comes to street vendors hawking concert tickets (especially classical music tickets), the less frill and pomp worn by the musicians, the better the performance. The more frill and pomp—well, you get the point.

However, many performances are worthy of your time—exquisite, in fact. Fortunately, we had sufficient foresight to purchase tickets to such a performance, which was given on our last evening in Venice. The group was a well-known Venetian ensemble, Interpreti Veneziani. What good fortune this turned out to be.

The performance took place in the gorgeous Church of San Vidal. The major offering for the evening was what is arguably Vivaldi's most famous composition, *Le quattro stagioni* (*The Four Seasons*). The performance featured four soloists, each playing a different season, with "a pinch" of Paganini and Geminiani thrown in at the end. This was a group of highly skilled, trained artists. It was a marvelous performance.

Early the next morning, we left Venice with this superb performance still ringing in our ears. Think about what a privilege it is to hear a composer's music played in the venue for which it was composed.

Mia Visione in Detail

———

"The world of reality has its limits; the world of imagination is boundless."
—Jean-Jacques Rousseau

"Logic will get you from A to B. Imagination will take you everywhere."
—Albert Einstein

THESE TWO QUOTES serve as a reminder of the formidable power of imagination. *Mia visione* was birthed out of the creative power of my imagination.

Both quotes mention limits within the world in which we live. The limit we faced with our violin's journey was knowing that while it got from point A (Italy) to point B (America), we had no idea how. There was nothing but a vast informational void. This remarkable instrument had "lived" in Italy for almost a hundred years, yet there was absolutely no history, no trace, no record whatsoever of its life.

As I began imagining what might have happened to it during that time, I realized that any number of scenarios could have unfolded.

So I began asking myself, "What if…" What if, for example, it had gone to Firenze (Florence)? Or, what if it had made its way to Rome?

And what if the Ceruti ended up going to Venice?

This last possibility was the most exciting of all. Conjecture, to be sure, but fascinating, and there were facts to support that hypothesis.

I began my quest by gathering underlying facts, which then ignited my imagination. These facts, stated below, became the framework for *mia visione:*

Fact: At this point, we knew the Ceruti had been "born" in Cremona, Italy, in 1810.

Fact: Cremona lies a mere 140 miles southwest of Venice.

Fact: Music was the heartbeat, the very soul, of Venetian society. Venetians both demanded the best and got the best performers from around the world, in all genres of music. To launch a successful career as a professional musician, you had to first conquer Venice.

If, in fact, the Ceruti had gone to Venice, it could have taken any number of avenues, as it would have been in demand.

For example, church music was a vital component of Venetian life. So, it is possible that a gifted church violinist may have played it in the service of one of the many Venetian churches.

Or, it could have been played by a violinist in one of the many opera orchestras throughout Venice. Because opera was all the rage in Venetian society, the demand for fine instruments would also have been high.

But it is also conceivable that the violin was privately owned. I have read more than once that when you walked around Venice during that era, you heard either singing or the sound of an instrument emanating out of every home, on every street corner—or I should say, canal corner.

Another possibility could be that it enjoyed a career in one of the numerous cafés, bistros, or osterias. When visiting Venice, one of a traveler's most enjoyable pleasures to this day is to sit outside on a beautiful evening in St. Mark's Square listening to dueling orchestras play back and forth throughout the evening.

One scenario I believe I can emphatically rule out is that it had been played on a gondola. Never! That world is reserved for tenors and accordions!

As my imagination continued to work, and as I continued learning about Venetian society, one plausible, although admittedly unlikely, scenario leaped out at me. I continued to nurture this idea as *mia visione* was coming to life.

Fact: Antonio Vivaldi was amongst the finest violinists and composers Venice and the world have ever known. He would spend much of his life in Venice. Many musicians and musicologists will agree that no one musician/composer has wielded more influence over Venetian music than Vivaldi. His most extraordinary composition *Le quattro stagioni* has helped secure his place in history.

Fact: Many people don't know that while he was a musical genius, Vivaldi was also a Roman Catholic Priest. Yes! In addition, his head of curly red hair earned him the added notoriety of being nicknamed "il Prete Rosso" ("the Red Priest").

Fact: History shows that despite the glorious art and music that Venice was known for, the city also had a disturbing, dark side. Venetians of Vivaldi's day had an insatiable appetite for licentious, hedonistic living. This lifestyle came at a cost, however. Unwanted pregnancies and illegitimate babies were just some of the collateral damage resulting from such a lifestyle. Venetian society's proclivity to enjoy "the good life," which they did to the fullest, created a serious problem. How were they to deal with so many unwanted pregnancies and babies?

Fact: The city chose to deal with this problem much the same as society does today. They provided options for its residents. Venice established several *ospedali* (hospitals), but four of these *ospedali* stood out. They were established for the sole purpose of taking care of unwanted children—primarily girls. Tragically, unwanted pregnancies were also dealt with by quietly slipping the unwelcome infant into one of Venice's murky canals.

Fact: History shows that these *ospedali* were in great demand. They provided a free and discrete alternative to disposing of an unwanted infant in a gruesome manner. A woman could quietly and anonymously place her infant on a one-way turnstile called a *scaffetta* (shelf). This shelf was just large enough to pass an infant through the wall into the orphanage, where he or she would be safe and cared for.

As an aside: The adage is true, "What was old becomes new again." As I was researching this topic, I came across an organization called Safe Haven Baby Boxes. The purpose of this organization is to prevent the illegal abandonment of newborns. Safe Haven offers a twenty-four-hour hotline for new mothers, and safe baby boxes for those who wish to maintain complete anonymity.

Just as in Vivaldi's Venice, mothers dealing with unwanted pregnancies can anonymously drop their infants into one of these safe baby boxes, and the newborn will be immediately cared for and eventually adopted out to a loving family. In my own Commonwealth of Kentucky, in the city of Bowling Green, a mother recently deposited her newborn into one of these boxes. Within ninety seconds, the infant was in the hands of professional caregivers and is now receiving the attention she needs and deserves.

Fact: At the young age of twenty-four, Vivaldi was appointed music master at one of these *ospedali*, the Ospedale della Pieta (Hospital of Piety). Under his masterful tutelage and training, these girls—both those in the chorus and those in the orchestra—would become famous across Europe—international superstars, in fact. Heads of state, including the king of Denmark, made special visits—pilgrimages, if you will—to the *ospedale* specifically to hear these girls perform.

Fact: What is significant about this is that the rich musical culture and environment Vivaldi helped create continues to this day. The Ospedale della Pieta is still open and doing precisely what it did in his day, caring for infants and mothers in crisis.

Well, once I had compiled and organized this series of facts, my imagination took off again.

Vivaldi was a superstar in Venice. He was not only a famous musician, composer, and performer, he was equally as well known for his work at the Ospedale della Pieta. So, was it possible that if the Ceruti had indeed found its way to Venice, it could also have found its way to the Ospedale della Pieta? Vivaldi had died in 1741, but the *ospedale* was still known for musical excellence by the time the Ceruti would have arrived. I found it captivating to speculate that the Ceruti might have passed through the *ospedale* on its way to America.

Mia visione began to crystalize as we thought about our next Italian adventure. I love planning trips. I find it relaxing, calming. Once Cheri and I have agreed on a destination, nothing brings me more satisfaction than researching the trip. I could make the argument that it's almost as rewarding as the trip itself. I prefer not to use travel agencies but choose instead to do all my own planning. Armed with a mouse in one hand and a glass of wine in the other, I can uncover vast amounts of information while I "click and sip" by the hour.

We were in the process of planning our second Italian adventure when we happened to watch a PBS special that explored the life of Vivaldi, music in Venice, and the profound effect Vivaldi had not only on Venice but the musical world as well. No single musician has had a more profound impact on Venetian music than he did. This special didn't just focus on Vivaldi the brilliant composer and violinist, but on his character as well. I saw the humanity and compassion of the man in his roles as a priest, a musician, a teacher, and a mentor during his tenure at the *ospedale*.

First, as a reminder, Vivaldi was a Roman Catholic priest. His nickname was "il Prete Rosso," due to his curly red hair. As an interesting side note, historical documents reveal he also had a fiery temper and could be very difficult and temperamental.

Those two roles, in music and the church, would remain significant throughout his life. Music and the church would be his guiding lights.

Second, unlike other composers of the day, Vivaldi wrote for an odd combination of instruments throughout his life. Many of his works were written for what was known as "less desirable solo instruments."

Vivaldi's music has remained so brilliant and irresistible that even to this day, countless elementary and middle school violinists have played many of his concertos, including his famous A minor violin concerto.

The point being that even from a young age, Cheri was aware of Vivaldi's gifts as a composer. However, I was beginning to become aware of a different facet of his character: his compassion. It was this aspect of his character that attracted me and became the inspiration for *mia visione*.

At the same time, we also became familiar with the respected Vivaldi expert Micky White. Micky is an Englishwoman who walked away from a successful career as a tennis photographer working at Wimbledon.

She has lived in Venice for several years and has assembled a remarkable, ground-breaking amount of research regarding Vivaldi. She has spent countless hours in the archives of the Pieta, scouring through original manuscripts and church records, many in Latin, which she reads. She is searching for any reference to Vivaldi that might provide fresh insights.

She has pointed out that Vivaldi would spend most of his life in Venice at a time when Venetian society had an insatiable appetite for music. This was nothing new, as Venetians had always demanded much from their composers and musicians—over the centuries, many composers and performers had spent their lives in Venice, feeding that ravenous appetite. But Vivaldi's output was nothing short of enormous—prodigious, in fact. He wrote sacred music, operas, and secular music. He wrote them all. His ability to complete compositions quickly was legendary.

In addition to being a highly regarded composer, he was also a *virtuoso del violino*—a violin virtuoso rockstar who enthralled and captivated his audiences himself.

As I continued my research, I discovered that at Vivaldi's Ospedale della Pieta, education was an absolute priority as the girls grew into adulthood. Interestingly, many of the girls not only grew into adulthood at the *ospedale* but ended up spending the rest of their lives there.

In addition to education, they were also given the opportunity to take voice lessons or study an instrument. If time proved that they were proficient, they could join the *ospedale's* orchestra. If a girl demonstrated that she was truly gifted as a singer, she might be invited to join the famous Figlie di Coro (Choir Daughters).

This was a big deal. In fact, it was a life-changing deal because this was the all-female chorus and orchestra that, under Vivaldi's guidance, would put the Ospedale della Pieta on the map, making it the most famous of the four *ospedali*. Because of that distinction, it played a unique role as a convent, orphanage, and music conservatory.

Adding to the girls' mystique and the charisma of their performances was that when they sang, they didn't stand in front of their audience as we are accustomed to today. They stood on the balcony of the Pieta and sang behind metal grates or grills, so the audience could never see them clearly. As you can imagine, this only increased their allure. Audiences were curious to know more about them.

Ultimately, this worked to the girls' advantage. Because of the aura this created, several girls had their own fan clubs. Apparently some even received proposals for marriage. They would never have had such opportunities on their own.

Vivaldi's work at the *ospedale* proved to be profoundly important. Over the years, under his tutelage, several of the girls grew up to become virtuosos themselves.

So, this portion of *mia visione* centers around this aspect of Vivaldi's work at the *ospedale:* his role as a priest and his compassion for these girls, his humanity toward them. He understood the humiliation many of them would have suffered for being in such circumstances.

The second part of *mia visione* focuses on his gifts as a musician. It has been suggested that Vivaldi wrote some of his most interesting works while employed at the *ospedale*, including works for odd combinations of instruments. There are plenty of theories about why he might have written for odd combinations of instruments, including that he wrote for whatever grouping of girls and talent level he had available at the *ospedale* at any given time. Others argue that wasn't the case. He simply wrote for these odd combinations due to the fact he was an enterprising composer. Whether he wrote these pieces purely for artistic purposes, or out of his care and concern for these girls, I cannot say. But *mia visione* certainly can run with this thought!

How wonderful it would be, I thought, if orphaned girls who had passed through the Ospedale della Pieta had had the opportunity to play our Ceruti. Even more heartening, however, was imagining that this wonderful instrument might have done then what it was created to do: provide comfort, fulfillment, and immense pleasure to the girls, just as it has to Cheri.

———

WHETHER OR NOT the Ceruti ever passed through the *ospedale* is unknowable. But that no longer seemed as important to me. What did take on new meaning was realizing that this red priest/musician clearly understood the girls' plight and had empathy for the shame and humiliation many of them endured because of their impoverished circumstances. By composing for whatever combination of girls he had at his disposal, perhaps he gave each of them a moment in the spotlight, a moment to shine. Again, provable? No. Comforting to consider? Without question.

As we planned our second trip to Venice, we thought what a privilege it would be to spend time with Micky White and learn more about Vivaldi and the *ospedale*. I was able to contact her via email and inquire whether it would be possible to spend the day with her as she introduced us to Vivaldi's Venice. She enthusiastically agreed, and so our meeting day and time were set. The rendezvous point she chose was in front of Vivaldi's Ospedale della Pieta.

Micky is full of energy. When she talks, her face and eyes take on an intensity. You can't help but be drawn into whatever she is explaining. She could not have been more generous with her time. She was excited to meet us and wanted to share as much information and history as possible.

She began our tour by walking us to a small, unassuming piazza well away from more popular tourist areas. In one corner of the piazza was a church, San Giovanni in Bragora. Immediately to the right of the church stood a home. Nothing special, certainly not a palazzo, just another typical Venetian home.

Micky nonchalantly pointed out that this was the home where Vivaldi had been born. She was clearly in her element as she watched our reaction. The church next door also happened to be the church where he was baptized.

She invited us to follow her into the church. The parish priest entered the sanctuary to meet us. These two clearly knew each other well and trusted each other. Speaking to the priest in fluent Italian, she requested a surprise that neither of us will forget.

With an understanding nod, the priest turned to us and motioned for us to follow him. He escorted us into the back offices and into a small room. He slipped on white gloves and pulled out an enormous, ancient-looking, leather-bound book that looked as though it could fall apart at any moment. This old book, along with several others, recorded the announcements of the births that had taken place in the church over the centuries.

Handling the volume with extreme care, he turned the pages until he came to the birth announcement of one Antonio Vivaldi, on March 4, 1678. Vivaldi was baptized in May of 1678. A plaque bearing this information can still be found next to the baptismal font. We stared at it in disbelief, but there it was.

Toward the end of our day together, Micky summed it up by saying, "I believe Vivaldi's music deeply touches people the way it does because he was a priest. Because he was a priest, he had a special connection with God, a connection that other composers didn't have."

Following our time with Micky, facts from both of our Venice visits began to coalesce. *Mia visione* was becoming more refined.

In the following days, I spent considerable time thinking about all that we had seen and learned. But I found myself constantly pondering the history of the Ceruti and wondering whether *this* violin could be one of *the* violins that had been played in St. Mark's Basilica or the world-renowned opera house Teatro la Fenice. Or, perhaps, just perhaps, was it played by some of the girls at the Ospedale della Pieta?

Was Venice one of the stops it had made on its journey from Cremona to America? While the answer to that question is unknowable, it certainly isn't outside the realm of possibility, and besides, isn't it captivating to consider?

Season I Author's Whim:
Rossini, Opera Buffa, and Tears

———

O PERA IS AN art form that is extravagant like no other. It combines orchestral music, singing, and acting into a staged extravaganza that has the power to transport you to another world. My experience is that opera tends to produce a strong reaction in people. Either they enjoy it, or they don't. There seems to be little middle ground.

Cheri has played many operas throughout her career: Italian operas, German operas, French operas, American operas, and contemporary operas—all as part of her professional duties. It is fair to say that she, understandably, isn't as enthusiastic about opera as I am. Why? Simply because the orchestra pits in many opera houses are notoriously cramped. This translates into confined and crowded conditions for the musicians. On more than one occasion, Cheri has been kicked in the head as first-row patrons stretch their legs a bit too far. The discomfort is further compounded by the fact that violinists rarely get a break, a chance to rest their arms for a bit. This makes it physically painful for their necks, backs, shoulders, and hands.

Nonetheless, attending a performance given by a world-class opera company in the venue for which the composer wrote it is one of life's rare pleasures. This was what we did while in Venice in June 2011.

Teatro la Fenice di Venezia is undoubtedly one of Italy's most glorious, breathtaking opera houses. Given my proclivity to do a lot of research before our trips, I discovered that the orchestra and chorus of la Fenice were going to be performing Gioachino Rossini's *The Barber of Seville* during our time in Venice.

Anyone who has ever watched a Bugs Bunny Looney Toons cartoon is probably familiar with this opera's music. It is what is known as *Opera Buffa*—comic opera, a farce. It is true that the setting of the opera is comedic. Still, in the hands of such artists as we saw that evening, it is nothing short of enchanting.

We were disappointed that the opera was not staged in the grand Teatro la Fenice but in the smaller, less opulent Teatro Malibran. Despite the less glamorous settings, the hall's acoustics were superb. Cheri and I had purchased box seats, orchestra left, for the evening's performance. It was a cozy box that comfortably seated four. The couple sitting behind us, who rushed in just before the performance was about to begin, spoke no English. That fact, combined with my inadequate Italian, rendered the four of us virtually mute except for lots of smiles and nodding of heads. We were about to experience one of the finest operatic experiences of our lives.

The production lasted a little over three hours—all in Italian with Italian subtitles, which struck me as odd. The conductor maintained absolute artistic control and conducted the entire performance from memory. In my mind, that alone was an extraordinary feat, more than sufficient to garner my admiration. The singers were of the highest caliber.

I glanced over at Cheri three different times during the performance. All three times she had tears streaming down her cheeks. She kept whispering, "They play with such joy." Such is the power of music.

After the opera concluded, we were too excited to head back to our hotel. Instead, we found a charming, outdoor osteria and enjoyed a late-night meal with wonderful wine and conversation.

SEASON II

Coming to America

_____

The Journey Begins

A PROVERB OF THE ancient mariners says, "No wind blows fair for a ship without a port." While we don't know how, why, or when, Cheri and I are eternally grateful that at some point, a fair wind carried this marvelous violin across oceans and continents, passing through centuries and generations, where it eventually landed safely in the "port of America."

Life is about constant change and our need to adapt. Whatever its former life in Italy might have been, this marvelous instrument was certainly no exception to this reality as it left Italy and entered Season II of its life. The changes demanded during this second season would prove to be the most consequential of its life.

The Violin Appears in America

As I THINK about the Ceruti or any other great instrument for that matter, I can't help but wonder, "Who owned it?" "Who's played it?" "Where has it been?" These are fascinating questions, but they are also critically important questions.

History and pedigree are of great significance and consequence when it comes to fine Italian violins. The more illustrious and colorful an instrument's history, the more coveted it will become, which in turn means the more money it will fetch when sold.

An example of how important this can be is seen when considering Nicolo Paganini's legendary violin, *il Cannone*. His exemplary violin was made by Guarneri del Gesu around 1743.

Public opinion has always been unreliable, fickle in fact. Such was the case in Guarneri del Gesu's day as well. For whatever reason, public opinion had determined that violins made by Stradivari were superior to those made by Guarneri del Gesu. This was all about to change dramatically, however, as would the world of violin playing, when Nicolo Paganini stormed onto the scene.

Paganini was a technical wizard and a character of immense fascination. The likes of his technical skills had never been seen before. Many consider him the greatest violinist of all time. Even to this day, violinists struggle with the technical challenges of his compositions. He also "raised the bar" and ushered in a new age of technical proficiency.

There is speculation that some of his technical abilities were due to the fact he suffered from either Marfan's syndrome or

Ehlers-Danlos syndrome. One characteristic of people with Marfan's syndrome is they have overly flexible joints, which would help explain why Paganini could easily reach such enormous spreads with his fingers. It is said he could effortlessly execute fingered octaves, which are very difficult for violinists.

As Paganini embarked on tour after tour, people became aware of his technical prowess. His reputation grew. But along with that increasing public awareness was the belief that what this violinist could do was only because he was in league with the Devil, having sold his soul to him. As a result, his other-worldly abilities earned him the nickname "il Violinista del Diavolo" ("the Devil's Violinist").

Paganini took full advantage of this public perception. The power of marketing was not lost on him; he leveraged it to his greatest benefit by dressing in black garb when performing. His trim figure, long black hair, and black clothing only played into his mystique. Audiences were dazzled by what they heard. According to written accounts, women fainted from hysteria as he played, similar to Beatles concerts some 170 years later

But Paganini had at least two serious vices, women and gambling. At one point, his gambling debts were so steep he was forced to pawn his violin to satisfy the debt. However, as fate would have it, a wealthy French patron stepped in and loaned him a violin for a concert he was scheduled to play. The violin was made by Guarneri del Gesu.

The irony at play here should not be lost. Here was a violinist supposedly in league with Satan himself, playing on a violin made by Guarneri del Gesu (of Jesus), which had been created to glorify Christ.

As Paganini played the del Gesu throughout the performance, he was gobsmacked, utterly smitten, falling in love with it straight away. To his good fortune, the wealthy patron was so overwhelmed by what he heard, he insisted that Paganini keep it as a gift, refusing to take it back.

In addition to its deep rich tone, this del Gesu had a booming sound. Thus, Paganini affectionately called it "my canon violin," hence *il Cannone*.

As for the audience's reaction, public opinion shifted immediately upon hearing what Paganini could do with this violin. People thought that if a violin made by Guarneri del Gesu was good enough for Paganini, it had to be extraordinary. And just like that, del Gesu violins were in hot demand.

Upon his death, Paganini willed *il Cannone* to his hometown of Genoa, Italy. Although it's not for sale and I can't imagine it ever will be, it is currently insured for $50 million.

Just an interesting historical note: It would be five years following Paganini's death before the church would allow him a Catholic burial on consecrated ground. There were two reasons for this delay. First, during the last days of his life, Paganini would not permit a priest to administer the last rites to him, refusing to believe he was close to death. Tragically, just a week later, at age fifty-seven, he died from internal hemorrhaging before a priest could get there to administer the last rites. Second, there was that pesky, lingering, perception that he had been in league with the Devil himself, no small matter when it comes to being buried by the church on hallowed ground.

This is an example of the extraordinary impact a rich pedigree and spicy history can have on the price of an instrument.

By contrast, however, as I was writing this book, the famous Hellier Stradivari, circa 1679, was being sold at Christie's Auction House with a starting bid of £5.5 million. However, when its lot number came up and bidding was set to begin, not one hand went up. The phone lines were silent too—not one bid. After several minutes of dead silence, the Hellier was taken off the auction block and, according to a Christie's representative, will most likely never be auctioned again.

In a piece I read describing this odd turn of events, a single sentence revealed that the Hellier had never been played by a major virtuoso. That sentence jumped out at me and made me wonder whether that was reason enough to make a potential buyer think that the instrument's pedigree didn't warrant the expensive price tag.

Regardless, I received an important point of clarification regarding the Hellier Strad during a conversation I had in May 2023 with Philip Kass, a violin expert and appraiser who has played a monumental role in our journey. I will introduce you to him in much more detail in Season IV.

Philip said that the violin is indicative of an early Stradivari. It is heavily ornamented on the ribs, the pegbox, and the edges of the top plate. Adding so much intricate and ornate inlay also added to the violin's overall dimensions, making it a bit larger than typical.

Philip also attended a concert at the Library of Congress in 1976 where a recital was given featuring the Hellier Strad. The soloist mentioned to him afterward that "the violin was heavy under the chin with a dark sound."

Was this fact coupled with the reality that no major virtuoso had owned and played it sufficient to cast enough doubt as to prevent the Hellier from selling? The answer is simply unknowable.

Regardless, the Hellier did not sell at auction, emphatically proving that the name of a great maker alone doesn't guarantee that one of his instruments will automatically sell. Or, if it does sell, it may not do so for the desired amount.

So, understanding and knowing the history of these fine, rare instruments that are hundreds of years old is vital. But it can also be an exercise in frustration—every bit as exasperating as attempting to research one's own family's genealogy. My dad was fascinated with genealogy and, as a result, avidly researched our family's lineage. But no matter how many different ways he tried, he couldn't discover our family history in Ireland before our coming to the United States. All these years later, the Ceruti would suffer the same dilemma. Honestly, it was both frustrating and annoying to know absolutely nothing about its early life other than the fact it was born in 1810. On the other hand, perhaps that is enough because, at the end of the day, we're both just immensely grateful that it eventually found its way here.

So, when exactly did the Ceruti arrive in the United States? Once again, we simply don't know. However, it made its first documented appearance in America in 1901, and that is where we continue our journey.

Throughout history, great companies have been associated with the great products they produce, companies such as Rolls-Royce, Patek Philippe, Steinway, and Louisville Slugger, just to name a few.

In the world of musical instruments, there is also a name that was synonymous with greatness: Lyon & Healy of Chicago. This company has been in the business of selling musical instruments since 1889. Lyon & Healy sent representatives around the country selling their instruments. That's right, traveling salesmen.

And that's precisely how the Ceruti made its first documented appearance in America: through a traveling salesman from Lyon & Healy. Apparently, a representative passed through Southern Indiana and stopped in one of its small towns, New Albany.

We don't have specific documentation as to how the two gentlemen met or how the sale was made, but a New Albany native named Mr. Krimintz—a local violin teacher—bought the violin in 1901 from Lyon & Healy. And just like that, it was on the radar as an American citizen.

Ordinarily, history would have no reason to mention anything further about Mr. Krimintz except for the fact that Providence had more in mind for his role in our lives. Mr. Krimintz would turn out to be a friend and fellow chamber music enthusiast of another keystone in our journey, the Hedden family, whom we were about to meet.

This is time for a reminder of the power of music, that it speaks to our souls in ways no other form of communication can. When words fail us, there is always music. It provides meaning and beauty when words are inadequate. It brings people together in common bonds of friendship and appreciation. And so, music and this violin would ultimately bring our two families together on the first leg of our journey.

A Grand Family

———

THE HEDDEN FAMILY was a well-known and highly respected family in New Albany, Indiana. They were also outstanding amateur musicians. Mr. William J. Hedden, known as Mr. Will, was a successful, already retired office equipment retailer. His brother, Mr. Earl, had retired from Floyd County Bank several years earlier.

As was often the case in those days, a proper, well-rounded education meant being well-versed in music, the arts, and literature. This was the case with the Heddens. Mr. Will was an amateur violinist, and his brother, Mr. Earl, was an amateur cellist. Their sister, Jenny, was a pianist. Most weekends found the Heddens doing what they loved most, being among friends while hosting chamber music parties and playing the music they loved.

Their friends included influential and notable names from the area, such as Hattie Speed of the prominent Louisville Speed family and the Speed Art Museum. Hattie Speed would often host these chamber music gatherings in her home.

As Providence would have it, Mr. Krimintz and Mr. Will became dear friends. Mr. Krimintz also became a regular in these weekly musical soirees. This continued until 1951, when Mr. Krimintz passed away. It was then that Mr. Will bought the violin. It would be his companion until his death in 1980.

Mr. Will's passing meant that decisions needed to be made and events set in motion so his violin's legacy would be secure and its voice heard for generations to come.

And so, in the next part of its journey, this remarkable violin would move from the life of an amateur chamber music violinist to the life of a professional orchestral violinist. It would travel all over the world: to the International Chamber Music Competition and Festa in Osaka, Japan, and nationally to such distinguished venues as the Piccolo Spoleto Festival in South Carolina and to Carnegie Hall and the Kennedy Center.

Change was definitely afoot.

Practice, Preparation, Laying the Foundation

———

"WHAT ARE THE odds?" I asked Cheri one day. "What are the odds that this violin, being born some 4,700 miles away in Cremona, Italy, would eventually find its way to Louisville, Kentucky? Add to that, what are the odds that a gentleman from New Albany, Indiana, would end up owning it while living in a home no more than twenty-five miles from where you grew up? Let's compound those odds by having a bank president hire me and bring our two families together, which ultimately paved the way for us to purchase this violin. What are the odds?"

Of course, I had absolutely no earthly idea what that number was, but the word *staggering* came to mind.

Excellence demands significant discipline, commitment, and sacrifice. There are no shortcuts, whether it's medicine, law, technology, science, or whatever the field might be. This is true of music as well. Cheri didn't just luck her way into a position where owning a fine violin would become a reality. Years of preparation—practicing, lessons, and sacrifices—eventually put her in that fortunate position.

Her background and pedigree aren't that unusual when compared to other professional violinists. However, she has had the good fortune to study with some of the music world's most renowned and accomplished violinists.

When I was growing up in the 1970s, John Houseman was a famous actor. He is remembered for many roles, but the one that sticks out in most people's minds is his role as Harvard law professor Kingsfield in the film and subsequent television series *The Paper Chase.*

In 1986, Houseman, wearing his trademark three-piece suit, bow tie, and white pocket handkerchief, made a commercial for the Wall Street firm Smith-Barney. The tagline caught everyone's attention when Houseman said in his pompous, thoroughly magnificent British accent, "Smith-Barney makes money the old-fashioned way. They earn it." And he really drew out the word *earn.*

The world of fine, old, Italian violins is similar in that they deserve to be played by talented, gifted violinists. This means when given the opportunity, each violinist must also earn that right. In the hands of less competent violinists, the true capabilities of these instruments lie dormant.

Since it takes years of practice and preparation to learn to play the violin in the first place, any violinist will tell you that finding yourself in the position to play such a fine instrument is a gift. In fact, it is a profound, life-changing gift. There are no guarantees that one will ever have the privilege of being in such a position to play one much less own one. It's a privilege not to be taken lightly.

Cheri's years of practice and her violinistic pedigree put her in that position.

She was taught the violin using the traditional method. She also happened to be enrolled in the first Suzuki group class offered in Louisville.

I have to pause for a moment to say a word about Suzuki. For any parent or student who has participated in the Suzuki program, there's at least one memory that I'm certain has been seared into your mind. In fact, so much so that your mind will never be the same. That one memory is hearing "Twinkle, Twinkle Little Star" over, and over, and over again. It's virtually impossible to get it out of your head. It's as if someone opened your skull and imprinted it on your brain.

It's very similar to the experience Cheri and I had while vacationing in Disney World back in 1978. As we strolled around the park, all we heard was that mind-numbing theme song, "It's a Small World," blaring over the loudspeakers in an endless loop day and night. Months later, long after our visit was nothing more than a memory, that tune was still getting free rent in my head and driving me crazy.

Over the years, Cheri's talent as a violinist continued to flourish, which brings me to another way in which Cheri and the Ceruti would eventually find each other.

It should come as no surprise to learn that the life of a professional musician is a world unto itself. Practicing is the axis upon which their world revolves, and it is relentless. There's a famous joke that perfectly describes this fact:

> A man goes to New York to attend a concert but gets lost. He spots another man on the street carrying a violin case. And so he asks, "Excuse me sir, can you tell me how to get to Carnegie Hall?" The violinist smiles and says, "Practice, practice, practice."

No musician is exempt from practicing. Some enjoy practicing and are obsessed with it, while others detest it. The world has known many great violinists over the centuries. Yet even at the height of their careers, practicing remains their taskmaster. Jascha Heifetz, one of the world's most formidable and famous violinists, was quoted as saying, "If I don't practice one day, I know it. If I don't practice for two days, the critics know it. If I don't practice for three days, the public knows it."

Cheri is very much a type-A personality. She's driven and disciplined, goal-oriented, and focused. Practicing never seemed to be an issue for her. She's always spent hours in the practice room learning and experimenting with ways to perfect a phrase. More bow? Less speed? Lower elbow? The art of violin playing is truly a balance of science and art, a constant interplay of physics—weight and speed—all to make a phrase sing.

As is true of any young instrumentalist, as they progress, and if it becomes apparent that they possess a degree of talent, the expectation to increase their practice time increases in direct proportion to the amount of their natural ability.

By the time Cheri was in high school, she was spending three to five hours a day in the practice room. Her mom thought this was highly unusual and certainly unnecessary. "It's not normal for a young girl to spend three to five hours every day in a practice room. You should be out with your friends," she would say. But it was too late for Cheri. Her passion for the violin was solidified in her soul, and she was smitten with its repertoire.

She was fortunate to have wonderfully patient teachers along the way. One was Peter McHugh, former concertmaster of the Louisville Orchestra and professor of violin at the University of Louisville. Cheri first studied with him while in high school. He was the one who helped her realize a fundamental truth about playing the violin and specifically about her playing. It proved to be a profound breakthrough for her. I'm referring to tension.

Tension is to violin playing what sand is to machinery. They are incompatible and cannot coexist. If not dealt with, over time, one will destroy the other. For three long years, Peter would talk to Cheri about the importance of playing relaxed, without any tension whatsoever. This continued lesson after lesson until, one day, a breakthrough occurred. Cheri walked into her lesson and announced that she had come to the realization that she was tense when she played. To this day, the two of them laugh about that revelation, but also about what a life-changing moment it was for her.

It was common practice in the 1970s for young musicians to gather on Saturday mornings for a weekly rehearsal with their local youth orchestra. Louisville was no different. Cheri became a member of the Louisville Youth Orchestra in the fifth grade. Young, talented musicians from the Louisville area would rehearse on Saturdays at the old Louisville Gardens arena. By the time Cheri was a junior, she was concertmaster.

However, she especially remembers one Saturday, when an important door was about to open. The rehearsal began in its usual way, except there was a crucial announcement. A gentleman by the name of Mr. Robert Tipps was visiting from the famous Tanglewood Summer Institute program.

Mr. Tipps was on a nationwide tour listening to auditions of talented young musicians who were interested in attending the Boston University Tanglewood Institute (BUTI). For anyone who's not familiar with the music world, Tanglewood is the summer home of the Boston Symphony and is located on a stunning property in the Berkshire Mountains, in Massachusetts. If not the finest, BUTI certainly ranks as one of the most esteemed summer music programs in existence. What happened next is proof positive that practice gives birth to readiness, and readiness gives birth to opportunities.

One sure way to make most musicians break into a cold, clammy sweat is to mention the dreaded word "audition." That's usually all it takes, and you'll have a front-row seat to a full-blown panic attack. Not so with Cheri. As is so typical of her, Cheri "just happened" to have a prepared program "under her fingers" and thought to herself, "Why not? Why shouldn't I audition?" With the energy and enthusiasm that is in my wife's soul, she eagerly auditioned for Mr. Tipps. The outcome—well, it couldn't have gone better. He was thrilled with what he heard and announced that hers was the finest violin audition he had heard to date in his travels across the country. Triumph! And with that, Cheri was off to Tanglewood for the summer.

This proved to be a pivotal summer in her burgeoning career. I remember a motto from my early years as a financial advisor with Merrill Lynch: "Success is a habit. Success breeds success." This was certainly proving to be true for Cheri. Her successes began building on each other.

That summer, not only did she attend Tanglewood, but she was also one of the concertmasters of the BUTI student orchestra. She would also be voted outstanding instrumentalist of the year. In one of her most memorable accomplishments at Tanglewood, while she was concertmaster, Leonard Bernstein was both piano soloist and conductor during a rehearsal.

As is customary in a symphony orchestra, the orchestra tunes before each rehearsal or performance. Anyone who has attended an orchestra concert remembers hearing the all-too-familiar mournful sound as the oboe plays an A and the tuning begins. It's also customary for the concertmaster to be the individual who stands in front of the orchestra and signals the oboe to sound the A. So in her role as concertmaster, she stood and nodded to the oboe during that particular rehearsal. Maestro Bernstein was standing near her next to the piano. Fortunately, a staff photographer nearby snapped a picture. The photograph of that treasured moment hangs prominently in her studio to this day.

A few days later, Tanglewood was celebrating the centennial of the 1874 birth of the famous former conductor and subsequent music director of the Boston Symphony Orchestra, Serge Koussevitzky. Cheri was again the concertmaster of the BUTI orchestra, which had the privilege of opening the celebration. As a result, she was introduced to Madam Koussevitzky, the widow of Serge Koussevitzky.

However, it would be a mistake to assume that Tanglewood was just about orchestral playing. Attending Tanglewood also allowed young musicians the opportunity to study with a private teacher and chamber music coach. Once again, Cheri's past successes built upon each other, presenting her with some wonderful new opportunities.

That summer, she had the honor of studying with the great Polish violinist Roman Totenberg. Mr. Totenberg was known and loved the world over as one of the most important and gifted vio-linists of our age. He was a kind man who took great interest in his students. He and Cheri became fast friends. In fact, on occasion, he and Mrs. Totenberg would have Cheri and her fellow quartet members over to their home for dinner.

Mr. Totenberg owned the famous Ames Stradivari violin. Made in 1734 (at the height of the Golden Age), it was his voice. For almost forty years it had not only been his voice, but it was also the only instrument he used to perform. I find it fascinating to think that Stradivari was ninety years old when he created this violin.

I believe it's a safe assumption on my part to say that as we age, we're less inclined to be as impulsive as we were in our youth. Case in point: During a lesson with Mr. Totenberg, Cheri did something I wonder if she would do today. She noticed his Strad lying on his desk and straightaway but politely asked him if she could play it. He clearly was a trusting soul because his response in that deep, rich voice of his was, "Yes."

She carefully picked up the Strad and his bow as well and be-gan playing. While playing, she asked him, "Who made your bow?"

"It's a Tourte," he casually replied. A Tourte! Francois Tourte was arguably the finest bowmaker in the world.

What an extraordinary moment! There she was, standing with a Stradivari in her left hand and a Tourte bow in her right. Heaven!

Many professionals agree that while Italians make extraordi-nary violins, the French make extraordinary bows. The two of them together are, well, perfection.

And it's worth noting that fine, rare, Italian violins aren't alone in breathing the rarified air of extravagant prices. So, too, do fine French bows, especially bows made by Francois Xavier Tourte (1747-1835). In December 2020, the auction house of Vichy En-chères sold a Tourte violin bow for $316,652. In December 2019, the same auction house sold one for $324,668. And in December

2018, Vichy Enchères auction house sold a Tourte violin bow for $367,862.

While Cheri will never own a Stradivari or a Tourte, her violin's music-making partner is an exquisite bow made by Eugene Sartory in 1910. He is considered to be the finest French bowmaker of the twentieth century.

Fine instruments produce gorgeous tones, colors, and sounds and enable the violinist to execute technical feats with greater ease than instruments of lesser quality. "Everything was so easy," she remembers to this day.

But what was about to happen to Mr. Totenberg's Strad would thrust it into the international spotlight for all the wrong reasons.

In May 1980, the unthinkable happened during Mr. Totenberg's tenure as director of the Longy School of Music at Bard College. Every violinist lives in fear of such an event. His precious Strad was stolen from his office as he greeted audience members following a concert.

Mr. Totenberg was convinced he knew who the thief was. Tragically, he was never able to prove it before passing away in 2012 at the age of 101 and before his "voice" was recovered.

In a sad twist of fate, in 2015, the police solved the theft and recovered the violin. It turns out that Mr. Totenberg had been right all along. The thief was a former student of his, Philip Johnson.

Johnson managed to conceal the theft of the Strad until his death from cancer in 2011. For the most part, he kept the violin tucked away in his basement. It was widely agreed that he was a mediocre violinist, but that didn't stop him from occasionally playing the instrument in public. So, while Johnson was well-known to his fellow local musicians, what they didn't know was that the violin he played was none other than what was known as the Ames Stradivari.

If there is a silver lining to this horrific story, it's that before he died, Johnson gave the Ames Strad to his ex-wife, who didn't realize the violin was a Stradivari. For whatever reason, she decided to have it appraised and took it to master violin maker Phillip Injeian in Pittsburgh. Injeian quickly identified it as a Strad, realized it was probably stolen, and immediately reported it to the FBI. That was exactly the break the authorities needed to solve the case.

The violin was returned to Mr. Totenberg's three daughters, one of whom is Nina Totenberg of NPR. In her book *Dinners with Ruth*, Nina Totenberg poignantly discusses her relationship with former Supreme Court Justice Ruth Bader Ginsburg, but also describes what happened to the Ames-Totenberg Stradivari after it was returned to their family. Rare Violins of New York meticulously restored the instrument over the course of a year, and it was then sold to an anonymous benefactor. According to an agreement between that benefactor and Rare Violins, it was then loaned to an aspiring young violinist. However, Covid-19 intervened, and the benefactor decided to sell the violin. The Ames-Totenberg Strad has been purchased by yet another investor, whose name is unknown, and the violin has yet to make a reappearance. Hopefully, that will change soon.

You may have noticed that Maestro Totenberg's Strad is now referred to as the Ames-Totenberg Strad. This follows an important tradition. Tradition has it that when a great violinist has played a great violin, upon the artist's passing, his or her last name will be forever associated with the violin. So the Ames Stradivari is now known as the Ames-Totenberg Stradivari.

I had the privilege of meeting Maestro Totenberg many years after Cheri attended Tanglewood. We met in Osaka, Japan, in 1993. Cheri and the Ceruti Chamber Players were invited to play in the Osaka International Chamber Music Competition & Festa. I distinctly remember the long and what seemed like a never-ending flight from Chicago's O'Hare to Tokyo's Narita Airport. We finally arrived in Tokyo but still had to catch another two-hour flight from Narita to Osaka. We eventually landed in Osaka and got settled into our beautiful hotel.

My memory of meeting Mr. Totenberg is as clear as if it happened yesterday. Cheri and I had just stepped off the elevator. We began walking through the spacious hotel lobby when seemingly out of nowhere, we heard a booming voice say, "Cheri Lyon from Kentucky." Actually, he said it with much more charm and wit: "Cheri Lyon from Ken-TUCK-eeeee." Of course, this was accompanied by his impish grin. I must say I was impressed by the man's fantastic memory. Though our time was brief, meeting him was an absolute privilege.

Paul Kling

IN THE SPRING of 1976, Cheri won an audition for a position in the first violin section of the Louisville Orchestra. She was just twenty years old. Her teacher at the time was Paul Kling. Paul Kling was a truly remarkable man and an equally remarkable violinist. He was the consummate Eastern European gentleman, exuding charm and elegance, and was always immaculately dressed.

Paul Kling was a key figure in both our lives. Ultimately, even if only indirectly, he helped us in the process of acquiring our fine, old, Italian violin. He took a keen interest in Cheri's progress as her teacher, and had I not chosen to come to Louisville to study with him as well, our paths would never have crossed, and this story would not exist.

While his given name was Pavel, in America, he was known as Paul. He was born in Troppau, Czechoslovakia in 1928 and always spoke affectionately of his childhood. I especially enjoyed hearing him reminisce about the crème-filled pastries he used to savor. He had purchased them at the corner bakery and later admitted he still dreamed about them. He also conceded that this pastry habit rendered him a bit short for his weight.

Both his father and grandfather were doctors by profession. His father, however, was also a talented amateur violinist who studied with the great Czech violinist and pedagogue Ševčík. He was also a composer who just happened to be a student of none other than the great Czech composer Antonin Dvorak.

In a memorial to Kling following his death, the publication

The Music Salon related a story told by Kling as to why he became a violinist:

> He used to tell a story about his grandfather and father. His grandfather was a doctor and had a good practice. He was prosperous and had a nice house and some land. Then came World War I, and after the war, they moved all the borders around and now his grandfather's house was in another country. His father also became a doctor, had a nice practice, and bought a house and some land. Then came World War II, and after the war, they moved all the borders and now his father's house was also in another country. "So I became a violinist."

Kling was a child prodigy—had a gift that allowed him many opportunities to perform, putting his abilities on full display. At age seven, he played Mozart's A major Violin Concerto and Bach's A minor Violin Concerto with the Vienna Symphony Orchestra. His first big break came at age nineteen with the Prague Symphony Orchestra, when he was asked to step in at the last minute for an indisposed soloist. The work for the evening was Brahms's massive Violin Concerto in D major. The rest—as they say—is history.

As World War II swept across Europe, Mr. Kling and his family fell victim to the Nazi occupation. Being that he was Jewish, the Nazis rounded him up when he was just fifteen years old and deported him to the concentration camps of Terezin first and then later to Auschwitz.

An article I read gave a glimpse into his prodigious talent. By the time the Nazis invaded their home, Mr. Kling had learned fifty-two violin concertos. He was also blessed with a photographic memory.

To feed his propaganda machine and to deceive and conceal what was really happening, Hitler created what he described as a "model" camp in a town called Terezin, set on a bucolic Czech hillside. By 1939, the residents of Terezin fully realized that this was no model camp. Instead, they learned the horrible intent of the Nazi regime as they were afflicted by one dictate after another, stripping them of their liberties, freedoms, and dignity. It was this concentration camp into which Hitler brought many of Europe's finest musicians, composers, and performers. Terezin was filled with music—opera, chamber music, solo recitals, and orchestra concerts—to give the illusion to the world that all was well. It was part of a horrible, evil delusion.

This was the camp into which fifteen-year-old Paul Kling arrived. His extraordinary talent as an up-and-coming international violinist was well-known even before he arrived. While at Terezin, the older musicians watched after him and nicknamed him the "Little Gifted One."

Mr. Kling never spoke to either of us about his experiences at Terezin or Auschwitz. However, his role in the Holocaust has been well documented. He also testified at the Nazi war trials. Prior to his death, he granted a few interviews. During one such interview, he said the following about his time in the concentration camps:

> There was no happiness. It was survival, as you know. Culture is very often a survival mechanism for nations, as it is for smaller groups...because, after all, everybody felt that there is perhaps more chance in surviving if you are unified at least in spirit if not in anything else. People had to sustain a civilized life under the conditions and needed something other than language. Culture was needed.

Mr. Kling survived the concentration camps and went on to build an enviable international career. Many consider him to be one of the finest if not the finest violinist of his generation.

Toward the end of his life, he reflected that he had been lucky with so many things in his life. Lucky to have survived the concentration camps. Lucky to have been able to own and play a beautiful

Cremonese violin made by Andrea Guarneri, grandfather of the famous Guarneri del Gesu.

A culmination point of his career came when he received the Austrian Cross of Honor for Arts and Letters in 1998, presented to him by the president of the Republic of Austria.

Mr. Kling was the reason Cheri and I met. We were both students in his studio. I first met Paul Kling in the summer of 1975. He was already larger than life to me—I had known of him and his reputation for several years. I was a violin performance major and had completed my freshman year at the University of Wisconsin Eau Claire. But I was determined to study elsewhere to spread my wings. I was aware of Mr. Kling and was interested in auditioning for a spot in his studio. After reaching out to him, we agreed I would send him an audition tape so he could assess my abilities.

Paul Kling receiving the Austrian Cross of Honor

There was that horrid word again—*audition!* I remember spending days agonizing over the audition and the preparation of the dreaded tape. I still break into a sweat thinking about it, although nowadays, a glass of wine usually helps assuage my anxiety.

I finally recorded the tape in 1975, which was in the days of clumsy reel-to-reel tape recorders. I wanted it to be—no, it had to be—perfect. But I had a problem. I was never fully satisfied with any one take. So, I concocted the brilliant idea that I should splice the best segments of various takes into one. Surely then I would be satisfied enough with the result to submit it. Well, in hindsight, I can now say this plan proved to be woefully ill-conceived.

Eventually, I sent the tape to him with a great deal of trepidation. All these years later, I wish I could have been a fly on the wall when he listened to the tape because it proved to be "inconclusive" regarding my actual abilities. So despite my scheming, Mr. Kling mercifully invited me to fly to Louisville to play in person. No more spliced recordings.

And so it was that in the summer of 1975, on a Saturday morning, I boarded my first jet flight ever, from Eau Claire, Wisconsin, to Louisville, Kentucky, where Mr. Kling met me at my hotel. From there, it was off to his studio on the University of Louisville Shelby Campus. This was a satellite campus for the School of Music.

As we drove up the mile-long driveway to the campus, we came to a sizeable grass-covered triangle where several music students were playing an impromptu game of baseball. Mr. Kling rolled down the window of his beloved BMW and said hello to everyone, and asked who was winning. One of the more energetic players said, "Come on and join us!" As I discovered over time, Mr. Kling had a wickedly fast wit. He immediately responded in his elegant Czech accent, "No. No. No. We are sissies. We play the violin." And with that, we sped off.

The following fall, I would begin my sophomore year at the University of Louisville as a student in Mr. Kling's studio. Little did I know that I would meet my future wife within a matter of days.

Life is ironic in so many ways. I was a young, naïve violinist when I came to Louisville to study with Paul Kling. I didn't fully appreciate or understand what a gift and an enormous opportunity this was. The truth is, I was too inexperienced to ask questions of him that, if given the opportunity today, I would ask and then savor his answers.

I have many lovely memories of Paul Kling. The three of us remained friends until his passing. Because I did not study with him for a full four years, nor did I pursue the violin as a career, he referred to Cheri and me as his "one and a half former victims." I loved his wit.

As for Cheri, Mr. Kling continued to nurture her talent, often teasing her, saying, "Violin is so impractical for long-necked beauties." As is true with any good teacher, he pushed her to excel and grow. Because of that, in the summer of 1975, another significant opportunity presented itself to Cheri.

Each generation produces names, great names that represent the best of different disciplines. In the world of violin pedagogy, that name was Ivan Galamian. He dominated this world from 1924 to 1981. So many great violinists of note studied with the man: students such as Itzhak Perlman, Pinchas Zukerman, Kyung-Wha-Chung, and Jamie Laredo, to name just a few.

Mr. Galamian was an Armenian-American born in Iran. After having permanently moved to the United States, he taught violin at the famous Curtis Institute of Music and was head of the violin department at the Juilliard School. During the summer months, he taught at the Meadowmount School, which he founded and where gifted students could spend either four or eight weeks studying with him.

Cheri applied to and was accepted at Meadowmount and spent four weeks that summer studying with this giant. Make no mistake, students were at Meadowmount for one reason and one reason only: to have lessons and to practice, practice, practice—end of the story.

At the appointed times during her four-week stay, Cheri would walk into Galamian's studio for her lesson, accompanied by an assistant. The assistant's job was to write down precisely what Mr. Galamian instructed, as if these notes were to be inscribed on tablets of stone the moment Cheri walked out of his studio. It was a productive and encouraging summer, and Cheri's successes continued to mount.

Fast forward to the following summer, which placed yet another opportunity at her feet. We went to college during a time when chamber music and especially string quartets were in high demand. The great quartets of the day included names like the Juilliard String Quartet, the Guarneri String Quartet, and the Tokyo String Quartet. To hear these groups perform live was breathtaking, sublime, perfection.

During the summer of 1976, Cheri was accepted into the Yale at Norfolk Chamber Music program. She would spend that summer studying chamber music in a one-on-one situation with the Tokyo String Quartet. As you might expect, given that Cheri's quartet and the Tokyo String Quartet members spent so much time together, they became close friends. In the years that followed, their friendship not only endured, but it was always a highlight of our year when they performed in Louisville. Following one Sunday afternoon performance, we had the privilege of hosting them in our home for dinner. It was a memorable evening.

Charles Phillips

———

THE NEXT SEGMENT of our journey would finally put us on a direct glide path to meet Mr. Will and his precious violin.

Early one evening in 1978, just after dinner, the rotary telephone hanging on the kitchen wall rang. I answered, and the voice on the other end said, "This is Charles Phillips. I know this isn't what we talked about this morning, but I was wondering if you could start work tomorrow?" His question

Charles Phillips

caught me off guard, but I immediately responded, "Of course!"

Little did I know that this man who I had just met for the first time earlier that day was about to take center stage in our lives and would play a pivotal role in making this connection.

A personal observation about Mr. Phillips. Notice that I call him "Mr." Phillips. We humans are odd creatures. Upbringing and habits are engrained in us. I am living proof that these habits stay with us even into our old age. For example, I grew up in Wisconsin in a family where manners were taught and were expected to be followed. Not "hoped" to be observed, but expected to be followed. This was especially true when it came to respecting our elders. Failing to follow these rules brought highly unpleasant consequences straightaway from my parents. Addressing an elder as "Mr." or "Mrs." was high on the list of showing them the courtesy and respect they deserved. That was seared into my consciousness throughout my youth.

As I write this book, I am in my late sixties, but no matter how old I get, Charles Phillips was and always will be "Mr. Phillips." Others might choose to call him "Charles," even "Charlie," perhaps—no one ever dared call him "Chuck"—but to me, he will always be "Mr. Phillips."

So, how and why did I meet Mr. Phillips? To make sense of all this, I need to back up a bit, to 1978, to be exact.

I grew up taking music lessons—both piano and violin. This was not uncommon, at least not in our family. However, somewhere during my high school years, I decided I wanted to major in music—violin, specifically. I eventually graduated with a bachelor's degree in violin performance in 1978 from the University of Louisville. However, during my junior year, I had an epiphany, a "come to Jesus" moment. When I was alone with my thoughts and brutally honest with myself, I knew in my heart I would never be able to make a living as a professional musician. I had a bucket full of desire but only a thimble full of the talent such a profession demanded.

Cheri and I were in a serious relationship by that time and making plans to marry. Part of realizing I wasn't going to be able to make it in this business was solidified when Cheri announced one day that, once we were married, and in order to enhance our meager income, we would both need to give violin lessons. I swallowed hard and said, "Do you mean I'm going to have to teach?" That is precisely what she meant. I was horrified—and I emphasize the word *horrified*. Clearly, I had not thought this through sufficiently. At that moment, I knew I had to conceive an exit strategy. I had to find a career where I could be successful and happy while making some money, too. Mr. Phillips unlocked that door.

So, with that as my objective, one week after I graduated from music school, I began interviewing for jobs in the business world.

I didn't have the heart to tell my parents until after I graduated that I would not be pursuing full-time employment using the degree into which they had just poured four years of tuition. But as was always the case with my mom and dad, they couldn't have been more loving, gracious, or unconditionally supportive, which I am thankful for to this day.

The thought of interviewing for a position outside the world of music was terrifying. I knew very little about how the business world operated. I had no idea what to expect.

I experienced the very same feelings the day my parents dropped me off at college six hundred miles from home. As their yellow Chevrolet Suburban pulled away from my dorm for the last time, I stood there numb and thought, "What have I gotten myself into?" I hate that feeling. I want to be in control, and I especially prefer that things be simple or at least as simple as possible. So, I devised a plan—a strategy of sorts.

It was a simple plan. I understood that accounting is the language of business, so I determined that working in a bank would make sense. It also seemed logical to begin the interviewing process by visiting smaller community banks in the greater Louisville area. I reasoned that this would give me a feel for the types of questions I could expect to be asked. Once I was comfortable with their questions and had sufficiently finessed my answers, I would then go to one of the larger banks in downtown Louisville and get a "real job." First National Bank or Citizen's Fidelity would do very nicely.

But on that particular morning in May 1978, God smiled down on me as I strode into the lobby of the first bank of the morning, the Floyd County Bank in New Albany, Indiana.

The adjectives best used— "green," "naïve," and "scared"—all were on full display. I didn't have an appointment. I hadn't even extended the courtesy of a call to say I was coming. I just showed up.

Upon entering the lobby, I walked over to the bank president's assistant, Lisa Moore, and announced, "I would like to talk to the president of the bank about a job, please." She quickly sized me up and said, "Wait just a moment."

I remember thinking to myself as I nervously sat waiting in the lobby, "What does the inside of a bank president's office look like?" After all, how would I know? I had never been in one. Honestly, it felt a bit like being called to the principal's office.

I envisioned rich walnut paneling and a massive mahogany desk with matching bookcases. Perhaps several Oriental rugs tastefully spread on the floor with leather-bound chairs and a couch.

Well, that fantasy didn't last long. The office I was ultimately ushered into was not large. It had no ceiling since the lobby's two-story ceilings were so tall, such an enclosure would have seemed ridiculous. There were no Oriental rugs, no fancy desks, and while there were leather chairs, they were modest, functional chairs covered in green leather, as I recall.

As I think back to that day, it can only be because she took pity on me and my ignorance that Lisa spoke to Mr. Phillips. A few short minutes later, out he walked. We shook hands as I introduced myself.

The most amazing thing during our introduction was that he didn't throw me out of the bank. Instead, he graciously invited me into his office.

Once again, God had just opened a door. While this was my first meeting with Mr. Phillips, I could not possibly foresee the impact he would have on us for the rest of our lives.

I intentionally use the word "our" lives because had I not met this man, I would not have had the career I enjoyed for forty years, but equally as important to our journey, Cheri would not own her

Cremonese marvel.

My first impression upon meeting Mr. Phillips was that he was a tall, lanky middle-aged man with a razor-sharp wit and a seemingly encyclopedic understanding of numbers and finance.

He wore black half-rimmed glasses. As we talked, he would peer over the rims, down his nose at me, appearing to size me up. Oddly, I never felt intimidated by this because he was so kind and was listening so intently. Every so often, he would take off his glasses as if to indicate that he was fully engaged and that I had his full attention.

This man, who surely had better things to do that morning, even if it was nothing more than getting a haircut, gave me forty-five minutes of his valuable time. He listened as I chronologically, methodically walked him through the last four years of my life and what I was hoping to do next.

Notice I used the word *methodically*. Cheri has another gift in abundance: the ability to be methodical and thorough. She is organized. Thankfully, she had spent many hours helping me piece together a coherent, methodical outline. I used it to tell my story, but also to ensure I didn't fall flat on my face or stray too far from the facts.

As fate would have it, during our talk, he mentioned that his wife, Pat, was a pianist with a degree from the prestigious Indiana School of Music in Bloomington. I was impressed! In addition, they were annual subscribers to the Louisville Orchestra. The thought instantly sprang into my mind, "This is going really well." Knowing this information was reassuring and put me even more at ease, but it also created an instant bond between us. He understood me, and I understood him.

He asked me about several topics but was particularly interested in the relationship between music theory and math. More practically, the connection between music and banking. You might assume there wouldn't be much of a connection between the two, but he knew differently.

He and Pat had obviously talked about this relationship, and she must have driven it home several times. He got it. I knew he understood because he concluded that if I was good at music theory, I would probably be good at math. But he went a step further by being willing to take a risk on me. And with that, yet another stone on the path to owning the violin—albeit years down the road—fell into place.

To my utter astonishment, Mr. Phillips offered me a job on the spot and asked if I could start in August. I was excited and so appreciative of the opportunity and the confidence this man had placed in me. I accepted his offer immediately and never took another interview.

I was a blessed man, and I knew it. The timing of his offer couldn't have been more perfect. Cheri and I were getting married in July, and none of this would interfere with or complicate that event. It was that very evening he called me to ask if I could start the next day.

I believe that we all have moments, crucial life-changing moments, defining moments when the split-second decisions we make affect us for the rest of our lives. This was such a moment. I believe with all my heart that if he hadn't decided to hire me and I hadn't had the foresight and courage to accept his offer on that fateful day in May 1978, this story would have ended then and there.

In the world of banking and finance, the 1970s and 1980s were a period of mergers and acquisitions. They were "hot." Everyone seemed to be buying or acquiring everyone else. The same was true in New Albany, Indiana. And so it was that Floyd County Bank merged with another New Albany bank, Union Bank and Trust, and became known as First Midwest Bank and Trust. Shortly after that, First Midwest Bank was acquired by the Louisville bank Citizen's Fidelity Bank, which in turn was acquired by PNC Bank out of Pittsburgh, Pennsylvania.

I still find it so ironic that in May of 1978, I began working for a small community bank with assets of about $70 million, but by the early 1980s, I was working for one of the country's largest banks—without ever having left my original job.

Following PNC's acquisition of Citizen's Fidelity, I lost regular contact with Mr. Phillips. But as is so true in life, the cream rises to the top. In the not-too-distant future, Mr. Phillips would be tapped by the governor of Indiana to become the director of the state's Department of Financial Institutions. He would serve in that capacity for sixteen years. I was so proud and happy for him. He had the temperament and the intellect—he was perfect for the position. In my mind, just like my dad, he was and always will be the best of men.

Meeting Mr. Will and His Fine, Italian Violin

———

A S IT TURNS out, Will Hedden and his siblings were dear friends of Mr. Phillips and his wife, Pat. The two families shared a long history. In fact, it was Mr. Will's brother, Earl, who had encouraged Mr. Phillips to work for Floyd County Bank in the first place.

I was still a relatively new employee at the bank when, from time to time, Mr. Phillips would invite me into his office after hours to talk—no agenda, just talk. I treasured those moments.

It was during these talks he would speak of the Hedden family and what "salt of the earth" people they were. The first time I heard about the violin was during one of our chats. "You know, Mr. Will owns a fine, old, Italian violin," he said with a sparkle in his eye. Knowing that Cheri and I were violinists, he was excited to share this news. Honestly, I didn't fully appreciate what he was telling me. But as is so often the case, time would change all of that.

"You know, Mr. Will owns a fine, old, Italian violin." The significance of that one statement must not be overlooked because it gave me a keen insight into the character of this man and his priorities. He cared about his customers. He took time to meet with them, to know them, and to listen to their stories. This was a role in which he took great pride. I can state unequivocally that this role was as natural to him as breathing. I've often thought Charles Phillips was a true humanitarian.

As my training continued, I had many opportunities to watch the man in action. Actions truly do speak louder than words. He was constantly helping bank clients with their needs. That could mean working with them to secure a commercial loan or apply for a mortgage loan, or simply helping older customers with routine deposits. No job was beneath him or his position. This made a deep, lasting impression on me.

As I've thought about those days, his example, and all he did, I've concluded that he was one of the first genuine "private bankers." Private bankers would come into vogue in the world of banking and finance in the ensuing years.

However, the world of private banking I was exposed to later in my career bore little resemblance to what I had seen from Mr. Phillips. This new world of private banking was one of low touch, high tech, where the level of wealth determined the amount of service rendered. I also observed that it was an industry fraught with turnover—lots and lots of turnover. To my mind, the very title "private banker" infers relationship, closer relationships than with other professionals perhaps. But this often wasn't the case. I could see the frustration on the clients' faces. Just as they seemed to be getting comfortable with their private wealth banker, that individual left or got transferred. Perhaps it was nothing more than a Human Resources oddity or coincidence, but their replacement always seemed to be younger—in some cases, uncomfortably younger.

The fact that Mr. Phillips not only knew Mr. Will owned a fine, old, Italian violin but also knew its history impressed me. He was always an earnest listener.

Mr. Will was well into old age when Cheri and I had the privilege of meeting him. Sadly, that one visit would be our only opportunity to spend time with him before he passed away. Cheri remembered that visit vividly and was later quoted by a local newspaper as saying, "It was a rare opportunity. He was just a marvelous person."

The purpose of our visit was simple: The Heddens loved the Louisville Orchestra, and now they had the opportunity to befriend one of its members, my wife.

Mr. Will and Mr. Earl had invited us to their home one afternoon. The home was a large, white, clapboard house that looked to have been built shortly after the turn of the century. Still, our visit was more than just social. Cheri had also brought along her violin to play for these two aging, music-loving brothers. Keep in mind, we still had not laid eyes on Mr. Will's violin. This visit didn't change that.

Although Mr. Will had been born in 1879 and Mr. Earl in 1882, during our visit we found them both to be as sharp as could be. They sat in front of the parlor's fireplace, Mr. Earl to the right and Mr. Will to the left. I sat to Mr. Will's right, while Cheri stood across the room and in front of them so she would be able to play for them.

However, before Cheri could begin playing, Mr. Will nostalgically intervened. He began reminiscing about how he still enjoyed taking his violin out of its case from time to time simply to hold it. After all their years together, the two had developed a symbiotic relationship.

Perhaps it's just my sentimentality, but I like to think that when violinists pass, they leave a bit of their soul in the violin.

In his reminiscing, Mr. Will lovingly recalled the history the two of them had shared. He never lost his admiration for the beauty and craftsmanship of the violin. Just holding it, he said, just having it close to him, gave him great comfort and pleasure.

An old adage says, "A clear conscience is often the result of a poor memory." I can say emphatically that while I do have a clear conscience, as I get older, my memory isn't always what it once was.

Sadly, with that confession out of the way, neither Cheri nor I can recall what she played for the Heddens that day. The one thing we both do recall is the delightful afternoon we spent in the company of these two gracious, kind men, engaged in stimulating conversation. It was our privilege. Even after Mr. Will's death, Cheri continued to visit Mr. Earl and play for him.

Several years ago, I read a book entitled *Who Are You When No One's Looking?* That's a rather ominous title that begs for some introspection. And so, in that spirit, and if confession truly is good for the soul, then I have something to confess.

As soon as we got into our car after our visit, we looked at each other and said, "Mr. Will actually believes he owns a fine, old, Italian violin." Keep in mind that we still had not laid eyes on the violin. But we both knew that his odds of owning such an instrument were small, infinitesimally small. In my world of finance and wealth management, I would have said the odds were statistically insignificant.

But as life so often does, it was only a short time before we were both served a huge piece of humble pie.

Following the death of Mr. Will during the 1979–1980 Louisville Orchestra season, and while waiting for Mr. Will's estate to be settled, Mr. Phillips approached me to ask our advice concerning the violin. His question was straightforward, as was my answer. What should be done with the violin while Bill Hedden (Mr. Will's nephew), to whom it had been bequeathed, settled the estate? "The violin needs to be played," I immediately asserted. Someone needed to play it in order to breathe new life back into it—to fill its lungs, so to speak.

He felt Cheri should be that person. And so, one afternoon at the end of the workday, Mr. Phillips invited me into his office for another one of our impromptu talks. He asked me to follow him into the bank's vault, whereupon he took Mr. Will's violin from its large lock box and gave me my first glimpse.

I was stunned. I immediately recognized that what I was holding in my hands could easily be a fine, old, Italian violin, exactly as Mr. Phillips had said. It certainly had all the classic traits.

Yet there was one additional confirming sign of an older violin that I have not yet shared, the grafted neck. You might well ask,

"What in the world is a grafted neck?"

As music transitioned from the Baroque era to the Classical era into the Romantic period, soloists were demanding more from violins. Certainly, by the time Paganini came along, soloists were trying to exact more from these seventeenth- and eighteenth-century instruments than they could deliver.

As a result, a solution was devised that involved removing the neck of the violin and replacing it with a longer neck that accommodated a longer fingerboard. The new neck was attached to the body of the violin while the original scroll was skillfully "grafted" onto the end of the newly elongated fingerboard. This enhancement allowed for longer strings, a somewhat higher bridge, and a longer bass board.

All these features added to the power, strength, and sonority of the violin.

As I held this masterpiece in my hands, the beautiful grafted neck was the last piece of evidence I needed to convince me that this instrument had a high probability of being a fine, old, Cremonese violin.

Noticeably delighted and with a smile on his face, Mr. Phillips handed me the violin case containing its precious cargo, and I proceeded to take it home to my unsuspecting wife.

Adrenaline is a remarkable hormone. Cheri believes it's a gift from God when it comes to

The Ceruti's grafted neck.
Photograph by Nathan Tolzmann

performing. Over the years, she has learned to harness its positive power, using it to sharpen the quality of her live performances.

But adrenaline is a two-edged sword, isn't it? It can also be an irritant, as it was on this particular drive home.

The words to an old Church of Christ hymn plead, "Fly swifter round ye wheels of time." Well, on this drive home, I was definitely experiencing an adrenaline rush, but the wheels of time weren't flying 'round very swiftly—at least not fast enough for my satisfaction.

The moment I got in my car, there was that familiar feeling when the adrenaline starts flowing. Your heart beats a little faster. Your breathing gets a little quicker and shallower. I was so eager to share this extraordinary moment with Cheri that everything seemed to take twice as long as it should.

When I finally arrived home, I quickly walked in the front door and climbed the stairs to our second-story apartment, gingerly carrying the violin in its case. Cheri was seated on the sofa in our living room.

Our living room was always most beautiful on a sunny day in the late afternoon, with dappled sunlight streaming through the sheers. It created a peaceful and lovely aura. It certainly set the perfect mood for what was about to happen.

She had absolutely no idea that I had the violin. I looked at her and nodded to the violin case I held securely in my right hand. As I offered it to her, she stood up, walked around the couch, and carefully took the case from my outstretched hand. It was a time-worn, leather-covered violin case, not exactly falling apart but definitely in rough shape. She lovingly laid it on the living room carpet, knelt down, and opened it.

After all the weeks, months, and years we had been hearing about this violin, this was the first time she had laid eyes on it.

Silence. Awe. Reverence. There were no words. Like me, she was rendered speechless.

Mr. Will had been right! We looked at each other because lying in front of us was a glorious, old, Cremonese Italian violin.

She, too, immediately recognized all the stunning characteristics that fine, old, Italian violins are known for. The beautiful golden amber hue of the varnish. The high arching front and back plates. The wonderful, flamed wood from which it was carved.

It screamed, "I'm a fine, old, rare, Italian violin. Show some respect!"

It had our full attention.

Season II Author's Whim:
San Polino, Vines, and a Violin

———

S AN POLINO IS a special place to us for many reasons. The winery is nestled in a gorgeous setting with stunning views of the Tuscan valleys and hillsides. Sitting at Luigi and Katia's table on their patio, tasting their world-class Brunellos while taking in that scenery, is heaven. The house is a classic Tuscan stone structure, and then, of course, there are the vines. Lots of vines.

The winery is owned by Luigi Fabbro and his partner, Katia Nuassbaum. They have poured their passion for winemaking into their land for years. They have made a serious investment in organic, biodynamic farming, which they're committed to. As a result, they consistently produce outstanding, award-winning Brunellos and Rossos. They are also kind, gracious, and compassionate people.

This was the second Brunello producer we visited on our daylong tour. I clearly remember the beautiful day and the exceptional views of the Tuscan landscape, but this was no ordinary day at the winery. It was *vendemmia* (harvest) time, and the grapes were being brought into the winery as we watched.

Ask any farmer or winemaker: Harvest time is stressful. Both Luigi and Katia had a very short window of time to pick the grapes, transport them to the winery, destem them, sort them, crush them, and get them into the vats.

And yet, here we were! I was just grateful they allowed us to visit on such a crazy day. Katia could not have been a more gracious host. We spent a lovely afternoon savoring their wines while she walked us through the characteristics of each. And all the while, we admired the Tuscan scenery. Of course, we shipped several bottles home and have been buying from San Polino ever since.

But there is a more intimate story to be told here. As I have previously said, music has the power to create bonds between people that otherwise might not exist. And such a bond was created between Cheri, Katia, and me, and it had nothing to do with wine.

Every year, Katia sends an email informing her clients that the current year's vintage is ready to be released. And so in 2019, I received just such an email announcing the latest release. The email spelled out the various packages we could purchase, or we could create a package of our own.

One thing anyone immediately senses upon meeting Katia is her compassion and care. And so, as is so typical of her, in her email to us she asked how we were doing and hoped all was well. I enthusiastically responded by placing our order.

But then I did something I still cannot explain to this day. I decided to tell her about a particularly emotional experience we had had just that past October, which involved Cheri, a very special violin (not her own), and a remarkable project called The Violins of Hope (VOH).

Violins of Hope is headquartered in Tel Aviv, Israel. The project was conceived by a man whose son has now developed it into an international mission. Now an old man himself, the son, Amnon Weinstein, is a Jewish violin maker. Today, Amnon and his son Avshalom, also a violin maker, work together and have turned the VOH project into a global undertaking.

The purpose of the project is straightforward: Find and restore as many violins as possible that were played in the concentration camps during World War II. The last count I saw was that they have found and restored sixty-four instruments. Amnon and Avshalom travel all over the world with them, taking them to cities and symphony orchestras. They spend time in each community so people can hear the stories of both the violins and their former owners and can hear them played. The VOH project had come to Louisville that October.

Both Amnon and Avshalom are fervent about this project. When visiting a city, they put the instruments on display for the community to see. However, the real objective is to get the violins out into the community. They don't want people to have to come to a concert hall to see and hear about these violins. Instead, they flood the community with several events intended to expose as many people as possible to both the stories and sounds of the violins.

Just as they have done in cities throughout the world, Avshalom planned to present several ninety-minute programs throughout the greater Louisville area, after which the violins would be played. The programs were presented in synagogues, churches, high schools, and so on. The week culminated in a concert given by the Louisville Orchestra, and yes, the concert included the theme from *Schindler's List,* with many of the VOH violins played by violinists of the orchestra. You can only imagine the range of emotions experienced by the musicians and the audience present at the Kentucky Center for the Arts.

Clearly, Avshalom could not do all of this by himself, and so, as is his custom, he had asked violinists from the orchestra to take a VOH violin for the week and join him as he presented his programs. Cheri volunteered to play one of the violins and was given the Dachau violin.

The name of the owner of the Dachau violin was Abram Merczynski. In August of 1944, at the young age of twenty-one, he and his two brothers had been deported from the ghetto in Lodz, Poland to Auschwitz, and then to Dachau. Amazingly, Abram Merczynski survived the concentration camps.

I was surprised to learn that at some concentration camps, being allowed to have an instrument was not unusual. In fact, the Nazis used the more talented prisoners for their propaganda purposes.

After the camps were liberated, many of the prisoners who had played during their time there never played again. The memories were too horrible. Abram Merczynski, however, did continue playing until he was an old man. At some point, he bought a new violin, and through a very circuitous route, what became known as the Dachau violin ended up in the hands of Amnon and the VOH project.

Cheri brought the Dachau violin into our home one afternoon, following a rehearsal. I can still feel the sensations and emotions that filled our home. They were visceral. She opened the case, and there it was.

We were very quiet, as the emotions were overwhelming. This violin would be in our home for a week, and while I could look at and admire it, I could never bring myself to touch it—almost as if it were a sacred relic.

I am quite certain Abram Merczynski, like so many musicians, had been used by the Nazis in their propaganda machine to mask the atrocities they were committing. I could only imagine the stories the violin could tell if it had a voice. But it did have a voice that Cheri would coax from it in a way words never could.

So, Cheri accompanied Avshalom on one of the school programs he presented.

A portion of Avshalom's presentation explained how emotionally devastating it was for his father to begin restoring these instruments. This was not because many were in horrible condition. It was because of something much more atrocious, much more unimaginable, in fact.

When Amnon began restoring the violins, he would remove their tops only to discover that many had human ashes inside, ashes that had drifted down into the f-holes of the instruments being played next to the crematoriums, where so many Jews had marched to their deaths.

Perhaps the most poignant moment, however, came at the end of the week, on a Sunday morning in our church. Earlier that week, I had attended a meeting with our rector. During our conversation, I described the VOH project and Cheri's involvement.

He was fascinated and very familiar with the project. In fact, he had just finished writing Sunday's sermon about persistent prayer in the face of overwhelming circumstances. He was planning to conclude his sermon with a prayer that had been scrawled on the wall of one of the concentration camps' cells by a Jewish prisoner who was executed shortly thereafter. It was a prayer of persistent hope.

He asked Cheri if she would be willing to play something on the Dachau violin at the end of his sermon. Of course, she agreed. So, on Sunday morning as he was concluding his sermon, he asked Cheri to join him at the pulpit, where they stood side by side. He read the history of the Dachau violin as provided by Avshalom. He then read the prayer that had been scrawled on the wall of that prison cell so many painful years ago. Then he quietly stepped back, as Cheri just as quietly stepped forward and began playing a mournful, grief-stricken, wailing Romanian folk song, unaccompanied.

When she finished there was silence. She quietly held the violin up high, over her head, as if to say, "This violin still has a voice. It still has a story to tell. Listen, lest we forget." People wept. It was a powerful, powerful moment.

Katia was very moved by this story. So much so that she emailed me back, informing me that her father was a Romanian Jew and that he, too, had survived the concentration camps, although with both physical and emotional scars that affected him for the rest of his life. Katia mentioned that his family also had a violin that survived the war and that was very special to them as well. It was played by his cousin and is now played by a niece.

Once again, forged on the anvil of pain and tragedy, violins created a bond between us that would otherwise never have existed.

The author with Katia at San Polino

SEASON III

Into the Abyss

———

The Violin's Identity Crisis, 1980

M R. WILL PASSED away in January of 1980 at the age of 101. His nephew, Bill Hedden, who would serve as executor of Mr. Will's estate, was a successful businessman originally from the New Albany area but now living in Kansas City, Kansas. I'm sorry we never had the pleasure of meeting him.

Shortly after Mr. Will's passing, Bill Hedden gave an interview to a local newspaper, during which he readily admitted, "I don't play the violin. It seemed senseless to put the violin in the safe-deposit box. I knew the violin was very old. But I was overwhelmed to find out how much it was worth."

His reaction wasn't at all atypical. How could he have known? Unless a person is directly involved in or at least aware of the world of these fine violins, learning about their worth—both historically and monetarily—often comes as a shock. So, it wasn't at all surprising that he was a bit overwhelmed trying to figure out what needed to happen with it next.

I am not aware of any conversation that took place between Bill Hedden and Mr. Phillips about the disposition of the instrument. But he must have asked for Mr. Phillips' opinion because it wasn't long before Mr. Phillips came to us asking for advice: "If this were your violin and you were in this situation, what would you do?" I knew instinctively what needed to be done, but I wanted to talk to Cheri first. I asked him to give me a bit of time and told him we would get back to him with an action plan.

At times like these, I'm grateful Cheri is such an organized person. She can visualize a project in its entirety and then create a plan that shepherds it through to its conclusion. She claims this ability is due to the fact she teaches. "Teachers must be thorough, analytical, and exact if they're going to help a student learn," she says. She's also very skilled at creating to-do lists, lists that spell out what needs to happen and in what order. This is exactly what the moment called for and what Bill Hedden needed.

I've often found that when people are stressed, it can be comforting—reassuring, in fact—to have someone take charge and tell them exactly what needs to be done. That was the role Cheri was now filling.

With our strategy clear in our minds, we met once again with Mr. Phillips. Cheri presented a plan, explaining what the next steps should be and their order of importance. She stressed that this was absolutely essential if they were going to be successful in selling the violin.

The first and most important task that required attention was for the violin to be scrutinized, evaluated, appraised, and "papered" by a violin dealer with an impeccable reputation.

Papering an instrument means that it has been thoroughly examined and appraised by a respected industry expert who then issues a Certificate of Authenticity. The Certificate of Authenticity gives the instrument standing and credibility. This is a critical step in making the instrument "legitimate" within the violin world. Working with a dealer/appraiser with an impeccable reputation is essential.

Cheri made it clear that no serious buyer would even consider purchasing the violin without it being papered. Mr. Phillips, who had been listening intently, responded, "Well then, who do you suggest?"

That question sparked a series of discussions that resulted in Bill Hedden making another fateful decision. Everyone agreed that Cheri's plan made sense and that she would be the ideal person to oversee the process. The only question that remained was who was going to perform the appraisal and paper the violin. Once again, Cheri had the answer: William Moennig & Son of Philadelphia.

Professional violinists cultivate relationships with violin shops that provide expert advice, authentication, appraisals, purchases, sales, and repair services. Having such a relationship is fundamental to the life and well-being of the violin and the violinist.

For Cheri, that shop was William Moennig & Son. Her relationship with the firm dated back to 1972. She trusted them completely. They were the gold standard in the world of fine, rare violins.

As you might imagine, the world of these precious instruments is not lacking for *luthiers* and repair shops. Many are legitimate, but sadly, many are not. For the task we had at hand, only a handful of shops had the credentials and expertise we needed. Because of this, Cheri was emphatic that Moennig & Son was the firm. They had an impeccable reputation plus the expertise, the respect, and the means to examine, research, appraise, and provide the documentation the violin would require.

With that decision made, it remained to be decided who should take the instrument to Philadelphia. That answer was also obvious: Cheri was the resounding choice. She was thrilled and honored to have been asked. And so Cheri set about making arrangements to begin the process.

William Moennig & Son

CHERI ENTERED THE Moennig shop exactly at the agreed-up-on meeting time. William Moennig III personally welcomed her to Philadelphia and to his shop. They exchanged pleasantries. But he was anxious to see the violin, so he went straight to work.

After holding and examining the violin for no more than two minutes, he looked at Cheri and said, "I don't know what it is, but it certainly isn't what the label says it is. It is not a Guadagnini."

Cheri vividly recalls Mr. Moennig making that declaration with great certainty and confidence, and her ensuing reaction. His statement was heart-wrenching! How could this be? How could it not be what the label said it was? It clearly said it was a Guadagnini, and now Mr. Moennig was telling her it was not!

He delivered the news with the same gravitas and conviction as a judge handing down a verdict of "Guilty."

It's hard to take in at first. Your brain doesn't want to process the news. Your blood runs cold when you first hear it. As I was not with Cheri on this trip, the thought that immediately raced through my mind when she told me was, "How does he know that?"

This news was devastating.

As the lyrics from a song by the Welsh band Lostprophets says, "It's not the end of the world, but I can see it from here." That pretty much sums up the emotions we felt at that moment.

Mr. Moennig's declaration had now thrown us headlong into the dreaded quagmire so many old, Italian violins are prey to—

forged, fraudulent, or no labels at all. I often imagine the excitement this violin would have caused throughout the violin world if it truly had been a Guadagnini.

This proclamation introduced an entirely new set of issues. The provenance of a violin is not unlike a mortgage title. All is well if the title is "clean." But problems—potentially significant problems—can occur if it isn't.

So, the question of provenance would be problematic if the maker of the violin couldn't be determined. If the maker was unknown, the worth of the instrument would be called into question. The Hedden estate could be facing financial implications—negative financial implications.

How could this possibly be, and how could Mr. Moennig be so sure of himself? So many thoughts flood your mind at a time like that, but we held steadfast to one truth: Cheri had taken the violin to Philadelphia because this man's opinion and expertise mattered. William Moennig & Son carried a great deal of weight in the world of fine violins. In fact, four generations of Moennigs had served the international violin community. Their shop garnered the respect of countless artists. Jascha Heifetz, Itzhak Perlman, Isaac Stern, Sarah Chang, and members of the famed Philadelphia Orchestra had all frequented Moennig & Son for their instrument needs.

Our Initial Moennig Connection

I N THE AUTUMN of 1972, Cheri and I were both serious student
violinists and juniors in high school. She was in Louisville, Kentucky, and I was in Eau Claire, Wisconsin. Both of us were already
intent on becoming violin performance majors in college. Getting
to that next level of proficiency, however, was going to require our
parents to make another investment in our future by purchasing a
violin capable of helping us advance to that next level.

While we wouldn't meet for several more years, I'm still amazed
that both sets of our parents, while six hundred miles apart, were
having the same conversations about the need to purchase new
instruments. It's equally amazing that both of our private violin
teachers pointed them to the same dealer in Philadelphia, William
Moennig & Son. And thus began our relationship with this wonderful firm, which would last well into Cheri's professional career.

Once Cheri's parents had decided to purchase a violin for her,
they sought out the help of her teacher, Paul Kling. Mr. Kling was
already a client of Moennig's, so the introduction was obvious. He
asked Moennig to ship some violins to him within the dollar range
Cheri's parents had authorized.

As was true with me as well, when the violins arrived, they
came with a meticulously typed letter from Moennig explaining
each violin and its cost.

Both our teachers made sure we only saw these letters after
we had made our choice so that the price wouldn't influence our
decision. During a weekly lesson, Mr. Kling had the instruments

laid out and said to Cheri, "These violins are so much better than yours. Why don't you just take your lesson on one of these?" Following the lesson, he told her parents which violin she naturally gravitated to, and that was that.

And so, on one magical Christmas morning in 1972, Cheri's parents gave her the gift of a new violin bow. Upon opening the package, she immediately understood what it meant and burst into tears. She realized they would never have purchased a new bow for her without first purchasing a violin. What a moment! At first, Cheri couldn't even touch the violin because she understood what a financial sacrifice her parents had just made. But there it was, a beautiful French violin made by Jean Laurent Clement in 1830. She lovingly named her new French violin Pierre.

Cheri owns Pierre to this day, but in the spirit of full disclosure, once this magnificent Cremonese violin came into her life, Pierre was quickly relegated to second fiddle.

While sitting at my desk one day, writing and thinking back on that visit to Philadelphia and Moennig & Son, out of nowhere, the word *kudzu* popped into my mind. What do Philadelphia and kudzu have in common? Very little, I suspect, with the exception, perhaps, of one small common thread.

If you've spent any time in the South, even if for no other reason than to drive the interstates to the beaches of South Carolina or Florida, you've no doubt seen an all-too-familiar sight: kudzu.

Kudzu is a pervasive ivy whose green leaves blanket themselves over trees, bushes, and virtually every other form of vegetation and life, including me, I suppose, if I stood still long enough.

Looking at it from a distance, the effect it has on the vegetation is to engulf it, thereby resembling a robe that has been draped over a person's shoulders. The point is, it's everywhere.

It's my opinion that certain cities bear some aspects of kudzu. Not in any physical sense, of course, but rather because the names of prominent city founders or other significant figures seem to be everywhere. Consider Atlanta, for example. When you hear the name Atlanta, what's the first thing that comes to mind? Peachtree! The name *Peachtree* is virtually synonymous with the city. It's everywhere—inescapable.

In Philadelphia, that name is *Rittenhouse*. It dominates street names, park names, districts, names of buildings, and hotels. Rittenhouse Square acquired its name from David Rittenhouse in 1825, but the family's history in Pennsylvania and the City of Brotherly Love goes much further back.

William Rittenhouse was a German immigrant who also happened to be the first Mennonite bishop in America. However, his fame and fortune came from the colony's first papermill business, which he began in 1690. It operated for over one hundred years. Mr. Rittenhouse, clearly an entrepreneur, recognized the colony's growing need for paper, and he seized the opportunity.

So it came as no surprise to discover that the shop of William Moennig & Son was located on Locust Street just off Rittenhouse Square, which is just down from the Rittenhouse Hotel, both of which are located in the Rittenhouse Row District. In other words, kudzu.

Locust Street consisted of a row of shotgun houses. While some homes were still residences, several had been converted into businesses. One of the restored homes belonged to Moennig & Son. The shop had a uniquely distinctive look about it because the first-floor windows fronting Locust Street were covered with tall narrow, wooden shutters with violins carved into them. The building had character and stood out.

For the duration of Cheri's visit to Philadelphia, she took up residence in a beautiful old hotel just across Rittenhouse Square, the Barclay.

This historic, elegant hotel has long since closed its doors to tourists and now consists of luxury condominiums. But during Cheri's visit to Philadelphia, this hotel, with its grand history, would be home for the next three days as her adventure unfolded.

Stepping into Moennig's shop was like stepping back in time. Bill Moennig III was a tall, handsome, elegant man. I have always been of the opinion that the shop reflected the same sense of refinement and sophistication as the man.

Upon entering, you were privy to a unique world. All your senses were instantly engaged. Your eyes fell immediately upon violin after violin, each one carefully cradled in suspended niches in the case against the wall to admire. Violins made by Stradivari, Guarneri, Amati, Bergonzi, and Guadagnini were also available but in a much more secure location. They were not for public display, for obvious reasons.

Your sense of smell also snapped to attention with the scent of varnish permeating the shop. I love that smell. To this day, it's a comforting smell and immediately takes me back to my childhood, when another smell, the smell of burning leaves, filled the autumn air. The effect on me then remains the same to this day; both smells evoke the most marvelous, comforting memories.

As I mentioned earlier, it was common to hear clients on the second floor "auditioning" instruments they were considering purchasing. But there is one other charming memory that vividly stands out. Even in the days of computers, the Moennigs typed all their receipts and correspondence on a manual typewriter.

Recalling our visits to the shop, I can still hear its clack, clack, clack. Cheri would agree, it was always exciting to receive correspondence from Moennig because their stationery was distinctive and every letter was signed by hand. Like their shop, their correspondence stood out.

Our relationship with Moennig & Son lasted from 1972 until, sadly, they unexpectedly and abruptly closed their doors in December 2009 after having been in business for one hundred years. From what I understand, there were two primary issues that drove the ultimate decision to close. First, the Moennigs cited the end of a generational line of succession. Apparently there was no one in the family who had the desire or passion to carry on the family legacy.

Second, however, was the reality that beginning in the 1950s, large shops like Moennigs were quietly closing their doors. Clients now preferred smaller, more agile repair shops that were popping up across the country as more people developed the ability to repair, appraise, and sell stringed instruments. Simply put, the concept of the large violin shop was becoming obsolete, and thus an era that both Cheri and I had grown up with and loved came to an end.

But on that fateful morning in Philadelphia, while neither Cheri nor I could have predicted the disappointing turn of events that had come our way, Moennig & Son was there to shepherd us through our crisis.

Laurentius Guadagnini was Lorenzo Guadagnini (1685–1746) of the famous Guadagnini family, another Cremonese violin-making dynasty. It's even possible that Lorenzo may have been a student in Stradivari's workshop shortly before Stradivari passed away.

All of this meant that the possibility of his having been a Stradivari student, coupled with the quality of his workmanship, Guadagnini's violins were in great demand, which, of course, drove up their prices.

But as devastating as it was for us to hear it, the reality was that this violin was not a Guadagnini.

For the next two days, the violin remained in the hands of Mr. Moennig while he examined, measured, and studied every inch of it to determine whose work it was.

Once again, this was precisely the reason Cheri was insistent that Moennig & Son validate the authenticity of Mr. Will's instrument. This is an industry fraught with pitfalls for the unsuspecting who fall into the hands of unscrupulous dealers. The adage is true: "If you think it's expensive to work with a professional, try working with an amateur."

Mr. Moennig was the consummate professional. Over the course of his career, he had touched, repaired, and studied enough Guadagninis to know when he was holding one and when he wasn't. We knew we were in the best of hands.

Neither Cheri nor I had ever been through the process of authenticating an instrument. Until this experience, we were naïve to the reality that provenance is a common problem. As is true with any valuable antique, the more famous the maker, the more famous the instrument's history and ownership, the more expensive these instruments become.

Fraudulent Labels: Revelation and Clarity

———

WHEN WILLIAM MOENNIG declared that he didn't know who had made the violin, but it certainly wasn't Lorenzo Guadagnini as the label said, he also went on to point out that the label was a horrible forgery. He went as far as to say it looked as if it had been cut out of a magazine. That added insult to injury! Those weren't comforting words. The truth is we were so far outside our comfort zone at this point we couldn't even see where the comfort zone was.

I had always assumed that the label inside a violin was like the body's connective tissue, forever bonding the two together. Without an authentic label, how could there be any hope of discovering who the violin maker was? This proved to be incorrect thinking on my part that was about to be corrected.

When my sisters, brother, and I, were growing up, we were expected to help with chores around the house. My dad often oversaw the quality of our work. After a few moments of observing our efforts, God help you if you got the dreaded question, "Do you know what you're doing?" That single question was the kiss of death, that moment in time when it was clear that, in his opinion, we had absolutely no idea what we were doing. This resulted in him schooling us on the finer points of how the task should be done.

As much as I hated hearing it then, I would relish the opportunity to sit through one more of his lectures all these years after his passing. I might even take notes this time!

Mr. Moennig could just as legitimately have asked us the same question, "Do you know what you're doing?" The answer was obvious. So we were schooled on several truths, including truths about forged labels, as we went through this process, which only served to increase our respect for the man and his expertise.

We learned quickly enough that the matter of forged labels had been a problem since the days of Stradivari. I was surprised to learn that even several Stradivari had fake or forged labels. I don't know why, but I took a great deal of comfort in that twisted thought.

Apparently, the forged labels of the seventeenth and eighteenth centuries were often so poorly done that they bear almost no resemblance to an authentic label. Experts can quickly spot it.

The most significant relief we experienced throughout this ordeal was coming to understand that forged labels don't present the nightmare we thought they did. My initial reaction to Mr. Moennig's declaration was seriously misinformed. Apparently, the label that's inside a violin is highly unreliable. As Kerry Keane of Christie's auction house puts it, "Labels are as changeable as a pair of shoes."

It seems it's much more difficult to find a rare Italian violin with an authentic label than it is to find one with a fraudulent one. Then there is the fact that many of these rare Italian violins have no labels at all. In the end, I discovered it makes little difference. An authentic label increases the value of an instrument, but a forged label or the lack of a label doesn't render the instrument unidentifiable.

This was so encouraging to us. Cheri and I both felt we could breathe again. William Moennig and his associate Philip Kass were looking at the tell-tale signs of the workmanship of the maker that provided the clues and evidence they needed to accurately authenticate an instrument.

This was an "aha" moment. We now understood. Experts like

Moennig have personally held, examined, and worked on many of these great violins over time. They've become intimately familiar with the techniques each maker used. Like a fingerprint, no two are alike, and no two makers carved their instruments in the same manner.

This was yet another reminder of why it's so critical to deal with an expert who has spent a lifetime handling and working with fine, rare, Italian violins. Because of their hands-on experience, they see patterns over time. They've seen up close the likes and dislikes, the preferences and quirks each maker had.

Stradivari, for example, created his violins in a very different fashion than Guarneri del Gesu. Stradivari preferred an elongated form of the instrument and longer, narrower f-holes. He also insisted on using only the finest wood—maple and spruce. Despite being somewhat of a miser, he was, nonetheless, an extremely wealthy man who could well afford to use such wood.

Just as an aside, purfling is an interesting phenomenon. When you look at the top of a violin, your eye is naturally drawn to the outer edges of the violin. It almost appears as if the maker has painted a thin, decorative, double-black line along the outline of the violin. In reality, however, this is ebony wood that has been meticulously trimmed and inlaid into the instrument's wood. It's not just for aesthetic purposes but serves to protect the violin from dings or gouges going too deeply into the wood.

Now consider Guarneri del Gesu. Del Gesu intentionally chose not to be the refined craftsman Stradivari was. His vision and concept of the violin were different. He worked more quickly than Stradivari. He preferred a shorter form of the instrument. His work had more rugged characteristics and was less refined. The f-holes were also elongated but often uneven. Yet despite these differences, his violins are among the most admired and desired in existence. They are every bit the equal of a Stradivari.

It's imperative to appreciate that these makers weren't being different just for aesthetic purposes or simply for the sake of being different. Not at all. They were in an obsessive pursuit to create violins that produced the sound they heard in their minds.

To an expert like Bill Moennig, these differences were immediately recognizable. Each instrument has tell-tale signs as to who its maker was.

So then, who made this wonderful violin that claimed to be a Guadagnini? That would take a bit of time to answer, and so it was time to hurry up and wait as Mr. Moennig went to work.

After his initial pronouncement regarding the fraudulent label, he began examining the craftsmanship of the violin in front of him. As he concentrated and focused, the instrument began speaking to him, providing him with clues as to its identity.

Over the next forty-eight hours, he found ample evidence to be able to identify and certify the violin.

"We were very fortunate to be able to make a definitive ID in this case," Cheri remembers him stating. With his research complete, Mr. Moennig confidently announced that Mr. Will's violin was the work of Giovanni Battista Ceruti, circa 1780. He was so confident and secure with his findings that he both authenticated and papered it.

While we were ecstatic to finally discover who made this wonderful violin, we would also come to realize during the process what an important discovery this was. We would also learn what an important role Giovanni Battista Ceruti played in the Golden Age of violin making.

———

ONE LAST WORD about labels. Had the label inside Mr. Will's violin been authentic, and had the violin been a Lorenzo Guadagnini, it would have commanded a much higher price, perhaps three to four times as much as a Ceruti.

During a conversation I had with Moennig associate Philip

Kass several years later, I asked how it was that experts like Bill Moennig and himself could be so confident in their conclusions.

Philip explained that during the first forty-eight hours, while Bill Moennig was scrutinizing the violin, he would have taken such factors into consideration as the overall craftsmanship of the violin, both the pattern of and the carving of the scroll, the style of the f-holes, and the quality of the wood, to name a few.

Philip also added that in the late 1970s through the early 1980s, Bill would often consult with the famed Italian violin maker and appraiser Dario D'Attili to see if he concurred with his findings. In our case, Philip recalls that D'Atilli did in fact agree that Mr. Will's violin was the work of Giovanni Battista Ceruti.

In the final authentication document, the Ceruti was simply described as "having a back made of a single piece of quarter-cut maple with generally horizontal, medium flames. The ribs and scroll are similar. The top is two pieces of spruce with a mostly medium grain. The varnish is golden orange in color."

As we read it, it seemed to be rather unremarkable. Nothing particularly extravagant. But look at it and you are seeing a classic, Italian, Cremonese beauty. It was as if this ordeal had finally introduced us to a new friend, an Italian friend!

Giovanni Battista Ceruti

W E LIVE IN a day when technology can place an overwhelming amount of information at our fingertips, instantly. If there's something you need to know or just want to know, you're just a few clicks away from satisfying your curiosity. If it's a person you're looking for, you may have even more information available because they probably already have a social media presence or even their own virtual reality TV show. You can at least go to Wikipedia and find pretty much whatever you're looking for.

Such is not necessarily the case when researching historical figures. For example, with all the information we have about the life of Stradivari, we still don't know where he was born or who his parents were.

If that is true of Stradivari, you can imagine how much more frustrating it is to look for information, any information, on Giovanni Battista Ceruti. There certainly is not enough to satisfy our curiosity about the man.

We do know he lived from 1756 to 1817. His birth, just outside of Cremona in the small hamlet of Sesto, also happened to coincide with the birth of the great composer Wolfgang Amadeus Mozart just ten months earlier. While Ceruti lived years after Stradivari and Guarneri del Gesu had passed away, he is considered to be a direct link back to the great Cremonese traditions of both makers.

Ceruti got a late start in life as a *luthier*. He did not open his own violin shop or even take up the trade of violin making until the age of forty. Prior to that, it seems he was a weaver. Even more remarkable, given the quality of his craftsmanship, is that he was most likely self-taught. Other than perhaps a brief period spent with the Bergonzi brothers, another Cremonese family dynasty, there doesn't seem to be any clear evidence that he formally studied violin making with anyone.

Experts also know that Ceruti used "adequate wood" but certainly not the exceptional wood used by Stradivari, Guarneri del Gesu, or other contemporaries.

Ceruti was well-known for his skilled craftsmanship, precision, and the beautiful sound his violins produced. The workmanship and way in which he carved his scrolls were consistent and greatly admired. The f-holes of his violins were symmetrical, and his purfling was beautifully inlaid.

Researchers also believe he was influenced by Guarneri del Gesu's models, as is seen in the craftsmanship of his scrolls. Like so many *luthiers*, Ceruti continued to refine his work throughout his career. According to the Chicago violin shop of Bein & Fushi, which recently had a Ceruti violin for sale, "Instruments by Ceruti are still in demand today and admired for their craftsmanship and precision, producing an evenness across all registers that is rich and robust in tonal complexity with strong projection."

Giovanni Battista Ceruti had a son (Giuseppe) and a grandson (Enrico) who were also *luthiers*. These three generations of Cerutis kept the Cremonese traditions alive.

Giovanni Battista Ceruti died at the age of sixty-one, most likely due to a typhus outbreak in Cremona in 1817.

What to Do with the Violin

N OW THAT THE Ceruti's identity crisis had been resolved, Moennig & Son provided Bill Hedden with all the documentation necessary to sell the violin. With William Moennig's signature affixed to these documents, the issue of provenance was settled. There would be no more questions as to authentication. And with that, Cheri returned home with the Ceruti, and well, honestly, that seemed to be the end of the story.

But it wasn't.

While working at the bank, I learned that Floyd County Bank's trust department had been appointed as the executor of Mr. Will's estate. And so his nephew, Bill, worked closely with Mr. Phillips to determine what should be done next with the violin to honor his uncle's wishes. Given the conversations that had taken place between Mr. Will and Mr. Phillips all those months and years earlier, Mr. Phillips explained Mr. Will's wishes, including the option of gifting it to the Louisville Orchestra.

What neither Cheri nor I could have known was that not only did Bill Hedden and Mr. Phillips put a great deal of thought into carrying out Mr. Will's wishes, but they also put a great deal of thought into precisely how the violin should be gifted.

Also, because Mr. Phillips had introduced us to the Heddens and because the Heddens had such a great interest in and love of the orchestra, their bond with the orchestra had been strengthened by our new friendship. Through Cheri, the Heddens now had a direct link to the Louisville Orchestra, which made Mr. Will's gifting decision seem even more endearing.

But unbeknownst to us, there was yet one more life-changing surprise to come.

Bill Hedden and Mr. Philips, along with the Hedden family attorney, John Cody, agreed that gifting the Ceruti to the Louisville Orchestra was exactly in keeping with what Mr. Will wanted.

However, these three gentlemen had gone further by including the stipulation that as long as Cheri was a member of the orchestra, she alone would play it, once again honoring the wishes of Mr. Will.

And so it was attorney John Cody who inserted this single statement into the gifting document, which would begin the lifelong relationship between Cheri and the Ceruti:

> At the present time, Cheri Lyon Kelley is a member of the Louisville Orchestra, Inc. and is using the above violin during her musical performance with such orchestra, and so long as she is a member of the Louisville Orchestra, she will be permitted to use the same for all times.

Because of that one statement, for the next nineteen years, the Ceruti was for all practical purposes on loan to her. And over the course of those nineteen years, it would become Cheri's voice, expressing her heart and soul. They were and still are inseparable.

This was an act of extraordinary human kindness and generosity, the likes of which you do not see every day. Cheri and I were overwhelmed, ecstatic, but so grateful as well. We immediately recognized what a life-changing blessing this was.

As I look back on that episode, it's in total keeping with Mr. Phillips' nature. Bill Hedden had carefully weighed his options considering the information Mr. Phillips had provided. He was sensitive to the Ceruti's rich history throughout the Greater Louisville and Southern Indiana area. It also made practical sense simply because, by this time, the Ceruti had spent almost half its life in the New Albany area. The New Albany community knew of its reputation because of the Heddens.

Bill Hedden's ultimate decision to gift the violin to the Louisville Orchestra ensured that Mr. Will would be honored and that the Ceruti's relationship and legacy with the area would be secured.

John Cody, Attorney at Law

J OHN CODY, THE lawyer who drew up the documents gifting the
Ceruti to the Louisville Orchestra, was a colorful personality.
He wasn't a passive participant in the gifting. He was an active and
enthusiastic accomplice.

And so, on October 13, 1981, by far the most significant piece
of the puzzle thus far fell into place for us.

John Cody and his wife, Beebe, were also close friends of both
the Heddens and the Phillips. Mr. Cody also happened to be the
Hedden family's attorney. Because of his close relationship with
Mr. Will, he was aware of Mr. Will's intentions regarding the violin. Armed with that knowledge, he wholeheartedly concurred that
gifting the violin to the orchestra with the stipulation that Cheri
alone would play it was precisely in keeping with Mr. Will's wishes.

The magnitude of this gift was something we could scarcely
comprehend and certainly never expected.

Over the years, Cheri and I had engaged in many conversations about wanting to buy a home while also recognizing that
she needed a better violin. We couldn't afford both. As a result of
this remarkable act of generosity, there would be no more talk of
whether we would buy a violin or a home. With this extraordinary
gesture, that topic was put to rest. So again, the question became
how did we get here and what did we do to deserve such a privilege? The explanation is as follows.

When Mr. Phillips hired me in 1978, he was the very defini-
tion of what a mentor should be. In my professional life, other than

this man, I've never had the benefit of working for a true mentor, one who understood and embraced the role. In that capacity, he was resolute that I should learn as much as possible about all aspects of banking. That meant hands-on training.

And so, my season of training began. I was a teller for seven months. I worked in the collections department for seven months (I'll readily admit, I really despised working collections). I also worked in the accounting/finance department. Along the way, I did a stint in the mortgage department. While I was never a loan officer, one of my responsibilities was to deliver mortgage documents and deeds to the Recorder's Office at the local courthouse and legal documents to the various New Albany law offices. I quickly became friends with several attorneys, one of whom was the colorful John Cody—he stood out. He was a founding partner in the law firm of Cody, Cody, Hay & Neeley.

Mr. Cody was well into his seventies when I first met him. He was not a particularly tall man, but he was imposing, nonetheless. His wardrobe was impeccable. He always dressed in a dark, three-piece suit, perfectly tailored, unless, of course, it was summer, when baby-blue seersucker suits were the order of the day. And to round out his attire, Mr. Cody's watch chain and fob were always in his vest pocket, adorned by a perfectly pressed handkerchief in his lapel pocket.

In the mid-1970s, anyone with a career in law, banking, or finance was expected to dress in such a manner. But still John Cody stood out. I should also mention he was a chain smoker of filterless cigarettes. It always reminded me of my grandfather, who smoked three packs of filterless Camel cigarettes every day. While I don't recall what brand Mr. Cody smoked, let's just say his smoking was prolific.

His wife, Beebe, was as colorful and kind as he and every bit as big a smoker. We quickly discovered they were lovers of classical music, enthusiastic arts supporters, and patrons of the Louisville

Orchestra. They certainly knew who Cheri was from all their years of attending concerts. The four of us were delighted to develop our new friendship.

Cheri and I were so honored when the Codys invited the two of us to their home for dinner one evening. It was a wonderful, memorable affair filled with conversation about music, history, and almost every other imaginable topic as well. Of course, there was the ever-present haze of cigarette smoke enveloping us.

During the course of our conversation that evening, we also learned that since Mr. Cody's law office was just down the street, he walked home every day for lunch with Beebe. The weather didn't matter. He looked at both of us with his mischievous grin and said, "We married for better, for worse, and for lunch!" You couldn't help but love this couple.

Our Identity Crisis, 1998

————

THE SCHEDULE AND demands placed upon a professional musician are stressful. This is especially true in December when Christmas breaks out all over. *Nutcracker* performances here, Christmas programs there. They seem to take up every waking minute of every day. During December, our friends find their patience pushed to the limit as we promptly turn down any social invitations with the all-too-familiar response, "I can't. I have *Nutcracker.*" Any orchestral musician will tell you the same. Cheri even owns a T-shirt with those words emblazoned on the front.

The point is simply this: While we had been married for some time and our careers were going well, we had never slowed down long enough to ponder whether life had anything more to offer than what we were experiencing. The calendar was our taskmaster. We were in a groove, a rut that demanded every bit of our time. It seemed as though Cheri was always preparing for a performance or giving a performance, which was beginning to wear thin. We finally stopped long enough to look at each other and admit, "There must be more to life than just this."

The answer to that one question dramatically changed everything in 1998. This was the year that ushered in an entirely new chapter in our life, a year that would demand us to make several difficult, gut-wrenching decisions.

From that point forward, we would now separate our lives into two blocks of time, life before 1998 and life after 1998. It was in 1998 our first and only child was born, Ethan.

Words are inadequate to describe our love for him and how he has brought such joy into our lives. In many ways, he has completed us. It's a privilege to be his parents.

However, that doesn't change the fact that Ethan was born with needs, special needs that would shake us and challenge us to our core.

In addition to being born with Trisomy 21 (Down Syndrome), he also suffered from a congenital heart defect known as a complete atrioventricular canal defect.

The doctors simply called it an AV canal. Cheri and I called it hell.

Only 10 to 20 percent of babies born with Trisomy 21 are also afflicted with an AV canal defect. We quickly learned to read his body language and his skin color. Those two factors almost always indicated when he was in or about to go into congestive heart failure. We became very familiar with Kosair Children's Hospital's emergency department. On several occasions, we either rushed him by car, or he was taken by ambulance to stabilize his failing heart.

I'm not a doctor. My dad, however, was an anesthesiologist, so I was accustomed to being around a world where I heard terms I didn't understand. Essentially, as best I can explain it in layman's terms, an AV canal defect meant that Ethan's heart had both atrial and septal defects. For whatever reason, the chambers of his heart didn't close as they should have during the heart's formation. It had leaks—lots of leaks. He had one large chamber when he should have had four.

Having only one chamber meant that each ounce he gained put more stress on his heart. It wasn't long before he no longer had the stamina to suck on a bottle of formula—it was overwhelming for him. It required his heart to exert too much energy. Eventually, we got to the point where any nutrition he received came from us via a large syringe and an NG tube inserted through the nose directly into his stomach.

I have learned over the years that nature waits for no one. There is a term used in the Neonatal Intensive Care Unit (NICU) for infants like our son who don't gain weight, can't hold their body temperature, etc.; it's called "failure to thrive." We grew to hate that term. No one needed to point this out to us. It was painfully obvious he was failing to thrive. Ethan was slowly dying in front of our eyes.

Not surprisingly, the day finally arrived when we were told the horrifying news that no parent is prepared to hear. If he was going to live, our son needed open heart surgery to repair the defect. But there was a problem. He was too young, and his heart was much too small. The doctors wanted him to gain weight and, if at all possible, they wanted to hold off the surgery until he was at least six months old.

It wasn't to be. We ran out of time. When Ethan was just three and a half months old, his heart could not keep up with the demands of his body, so open-heart surgery was required immediately.

In September 1998, Ethan underwent open heart surgery. His heart was the size of a walnut. During his surgery, he was placed on a heart-lung bypass machine. At some point during those two hours, he suffered two small strokes, one in the thalamus and one in the left caudate nucleus. Post-surgery, both his lungs filled with fluid and infection. When the fluid was drained, both lungs collapsed. Myriad other complications followed as you would expect from such a serious surgery. But despite all of that, and by the grace of God, he survived, thanks to his pediatric cardiac surgeon, his intensivist, and his team of specialists.

As Ethan grew, it also became clear that while he was verbal, he was non-conversant. To this day, our son cannot tell us if he has a headache or if his stomach hurts. He will occasionally tell us "Stay home. Too much sick," but can describe nothing further. Yet out of all this came one of the most important, life-changing lessons I needed to learn: the need to slow down.

I came to realize that if I was going to have a meaningful relationship with him, I needed to embrace and accept the reality that it was not possible for him to come into our world. Instead, I needed to go into his world. That meant slowing down and spending more time with him doing things on his schedule, in his time, not mine.

I soon discovered he lives in a fascinating, joyful world where he is happy and fulfilled. At that point, everything took a back seat—including my career—in order to give this amazing person, this gift, the life he so richly deserved.

Having said that, it still didn't change the fact that we were overwhelmed. What happened next laid the groundwork for the dilemma that would fester over the next two years and eventually erupt.

We found ourselves immersed in a world of seemingly endless months of doctor's appointments, in-home therapy, physical therapy, occupational therapy, and speech therapy.

Cheri and I were mounting an all-out offensive using all the weapons at our disposal. Our arsenal of weapons is what is known in the special needs world as "early intervention." All of this was being done in a desperate effort on our part to provide him with every opportunity that would enable him to grow into the healthiest, most successful person he could be.

Thankfully, Cheri and I have always been in lockstep with each other in sharing our son's responsibilities. But even with that, the non-stop demands of caring for a highly involved special needs son, coupled with the non-stop demands of being a professional orchestral violinist, proved overwhelming. Shirking responsibilities, slacking off for a bit, easing up on the gas pedal, even for a moment, was simply impossible. We were exhausted.

And so, it's no surprise that this all-encompassing schedule was devouring us and ultimately came to a head in 2000.

Coming to this moment was especially painful because we

both knew what the consequences of the next decision would be.

Cheri began seriously talking about walking away from her career with the Louisville Orchestra in order to care for Ethan. If she were to resign, the consequences were clear: The Ceruti would have to be returned. We remembered the clause Mr. Cody had inserted into the contract that gifted the Ceruti to the Louisville Orchestra, "and so long as she is a member of the Louisville Orchestra, she will be permitted to use the same for all times."

Neither of us needed to be reminded. That clause was becoming a two-edged sword. We understood that if she left the orchestra, she would also lose the Ceruti. That thought was unimaginable and too painful to bear.

With no way out, our crisis erupted.

It was a Friday afternoon—that day is forever seared into my memory. She had made her decision, made up her mind. She was resolute. She was going to resign. Now she had to come to grips with her greatest fear, relinquishing her voice, the Ceruti. This was equivalent to having a loved one ripped away from you, or so it seemed.

Occasionally life allows us a glimpse of raw human emotion. I witnessed this when I came home after work on that fateful Friday afternoon.

The pain, the horrible emotional pain, was etched on Cheri's face. She was sitting on the couch in our great room, sobbing, uncontrollably sobbing. Moments earlier, she had called the orchestra's executive director to inform him of her decision to resign. Her new role in life was to be that of a full-time mom and caregiver to our son. It's one of those moments you cannot unsee.

A wise person once said, "Words are the flesh of our thoughts." That may be true, but words are wholly inadequate to describe the pain I saw. Resigning from the orchestra was painful enough, but after nineteen years, having to give up the Ceruti was inconceivable, unthinkable.

The reality was, when we moved into our new home in 1998, we realized we had the stability of being in the home that we wanted. We committed to each other that this home was more than sufficient to meet our needs, now and into the future.

With that issue settled, we could turn our full attention to the matter of buying a violin for Cheri. We both understood that someday Cheri would resign or retire from the orchestra. Either way, she would need a new instrument of her own. And so we had reached out to William Moennig & Son to explore the possibilities.

However, it quickly became evident that something was amiss. Buying a violin should be exciting, but the fact was, the moment was devoid of any real enthusiasm or excitement on Cheri's part. It didn't take long for me to understand one irrefutable truth: The Ceruti was her voice. No other violin was going to replace that.

She and I spoke at length about this and ultimately realized that the ideal solution would be for us to take the bold step of offering to buy the Ceruti from the orchestra. But there were so many unknowns. When would be the ideal time for us to make such an offer? Would the board of directors even entertain such an offer? But most importantly, what would it cost?

There is an upsetting reality that musicians must face. In the world of fine and rare instruments, most musicians can no longer afford to purchase them. The instruments are astronomically expensive and, thus, entirely out of the question on a musician's salary. No sane lending institution would even consider making a loan for such a purchase.

What a tragedy that for the very players these instruments were created for, they are unattainable without a wealthy sponsor or funding source. I was well aware of this reality. To make this happen, we were going to have to determine what sacrifices we were willing to make to own this violin, this investment.

Cheri and I are similar in that we are not prone to making

decisions quickly or haphazardly. We need time to let ideas marinate—percolate, if you will. This was perfectly natural for me because when it came to making decisions, my parents were Olympic champions at waiting, percolating, and marinating.

That is until I came home that fateful Friday afternoon and watched what was unfolding before me. Something needed to give, and decisions needed to be made immediately.

Cheri has very keen instincts. Always has. Far superior to mine. I often remind her, "Trust your instincts." I rarely tell her what I think she should do.

But just as if it happened yesterday, I recall sitting down on the couch beside her and saying, "Cheri, you need to call back the executive director immediately and rescind your resignation. You're a better mom, a better wife, and a better person when you're using the gifts that God created you to use."

While we both knew instinctively this was the right decision for all of us, our dilemma now was figuring out a way forward, finding a new footing that would provide a new degree of balance in our lives. Cheri needed the flexibility necessary for her to be fulfilled while using her gift.

At that moment, I felt deep in my soul that it would work out, but I had no earthly clue how. None of that mattered now; we were determined to figure it out. With that, she picked up the phone and rescinded her resignation. As you might imagine, the executive director was thrilled.

Out of that painful, gut-wrenching episode came another life-changing decision. We determined right then and there to do whatever we could to buy the Ceruti and make it a permanent member of our family.

Season III Author's Whim: "The Fat"

BOLOGNA, ITALY! THIS glorious medieval city has been aptly nicknamed "La Grassa" ("The Fat One"), typically truncated simply to "The Fat." Over the centuries, Bologna has shared three nicknames. "La Dotta" ("The Learned") was the first because of the university located in the city, which also just happens to be the oldest continuously running university in the Western World. It boasts such alumni as Dante, Petrarch, and four popes, to name a few.

The second nickname was "La Rossa" ("The Red"), due primarily to the fact Bologna has always been a left-leaning city. You can easily trace this common thread throughout its history, beginning in the twelfth century. According to *The Local Italy*, research, Bologna has been left leaning "almost as long as it's been a city: during the Holy Roman Empire, it was a free commune. From the twelfth century onwards, it began to expand and became an industrial hub, giving rise to workers' movements. During World War II, it was at the heart of the Resistance movement, and was a stronghold for Italy's Communist Party for several decades after that."

But the nickname "The Fat" is what whets the appetites of countless residents and visitors. Bologna has had such an impact on Italy's food that it is considered Italy's gastronomic, culinary capital. Located in the region of Emilia-Romagna, it is the ultimate foodies' paradise. So what could possibly be more perfect than the two of us taking a private cooking class in The Fat?

But before I describe our visit to Bologna, I need to tell you about our experience getting to Bologna.

Just five years earlier I had already made the horrendous mistake of attempting to drive in Florence—a traumatic event of such magnitude I really should still be in therapy. But in 2008, we were staying in the beautiful hamlet and elegant boutique hotel Borgo San Felice. This is a peaceful corner of the world nestled in the Chianti region of Tuscany. It served as the perfect base for us to explore Chianti.

Driving around the Tuscan countryside is pure joy and relatively stress-free. But as with all good things, our time at Borgo San Felice came to an end. Our next stop was Bologna. The day leading up to our departure, I carefully studied the maps of the city, not wanting to repeat the disaster that was driving in Florence. The maps made the trip look perfectly doable. After all, Bologna wasn't the size of Florence, so what could go wrong?

With great confidence, we set off for Bologna early the following day. What happened next could be called "Driving in Florence—the Nightmare Sequel."

Driving to Bologna was easy—enjoyable, actually. But once I got into the city's historic center, nothing made sense. We attempted to use our map to navigate our way through the city—GPS was of no use whatsoever. But just as we realized where the map was telling us we should be, I would fly past the very street I should have turned onto. Notice how carefully I have chosen my pronouns, especially *I* instead of *we*. This is because Cheri is a terrific navigator, but my intercity driving skills proved woefully less than proficient, resulting in me getting us totally lost.

Cars, Vespas, buses, and taxis were whizzing around us in a flurry, as only Italian drivers can. With my nerves sufficiently frayed, I finally admitted I was hopelessly lost with virtually no chance of finding our hotel.

I pulled to the curb, stopped the car, and called our hotel. A very gracious host took pity on my plight and gave me a brilliant suggestion: "Look for the nearest *tassi* (taxi) stand," she said, which most likely would be close to a hotel.

I took her advice and found a taxi stand with several taxis waiting in line. She had suggested that once I found the taxi stand, I should ask a taxi driver to drive to the hotel while I followed in my car. Genius! I was ready to marry this woman.

I ran over to the first taxi in the queue and explained my plight in a combination of English and botched Italian. Fortunately, she understood the gist of my request.

But I also realized that by asking her to help us, she would lose her place in the queue, thereby forfeiting a fare. So I put a fifty-euro bill in her hand, which seemed to set her back. The fact is, she was willing to guide us to our hotel for free, and thus she strenuously objected to the fifty euros I handed her. I would hear none of it. I returned to my car, put it into drive, carefully eased in behind her cab, and proudly followed her through the narrow streets of Bologna, past piazzas, shops, ristoranti, and churches, just as if I had lived there my entire life.

Once at our hotel, we waved a long, grateful thank you as she pulled away. I'm sure she thought we were crazy Americans. But I'd probably still be hopelessly lost, driving around Bologna, had she not helped us.

Another life lesson: Never, never, never drive in a large city in Italy. Never!

We had come to The Fat for several reasons, none more important than our desire to take a private cooking course. After all, with a nickname like that, who could resist such a temptation? Once again, I had done my homework and found the perfect chef to shepherd our day.

Her name was Carmelita. She was prompt, as were we, and so the tour began. She was knowledgeable, and she seemed to know every aspect of Italian cuisine and traditions.

To our surprise, our first stop was a chocolate shop. I quickly surmised that chocolate was just the energy boost we needed—it requires energy to stroll the markets. You know it's going to be a great day when you begin with chocolate.

From there, Carmelita took us to her favorite market stalls and shops. Along the way, we passed vendors selling vegetables, fresh fish, fresh meat, cured meat, horse meat (we increased our gait past this shop), fresh fruits, jams, homemade pasta, cheeses, and balsamic vinegar. As far as we were concerned, "The Fat" was the perfect nickname for this magnificent city.

As we strolled and shopped, Carmelita explained the differences in the types of fresh produce we were buying. She had a very endearing habit. Immediately following each explanation, she would swoop up the fresh produce and hold it to her nose while inhaling deeply. With her eyes closed, she was taking in the fragrance, evaluating the quality of the produce. This woman had passione!

From the produce stalls, we made our way to her favorite *venditore di formaggi* (cheesemonger). The aromas coming from this shop were intoxicating. As you would expect, the selection was enormous. However, we eventually managed to make our choices, and then it was off to the baker for *pane* (bread).

We next headed for the butcher, with a loaf of fresh bread safely tucked under my arm. Our desired meat selection had been a topic of conversation for several weeks leading up to our visit. Chicken or rabbit? Having had minimal culinary experience with rabbit, we decided to live on the edge—rabbit it was.

But our culinary tour of The Fat was by no means over. Carmelita took us to her favorite wine store. After carefully surveying and discussing the inventory, we settled on three different red wines of the region.

The last stop of our culinary market tour was a Balsamic shop. This proved to be heaven. We tasted eight-year-old, ten-year-old, twenty-five-year-old, and forty-year-old balsamic vinegar. They were thick, syrupy, and so delicious that we took a bottle or two home with us. This was our first serious purchase of balsamic vinegar. We have saved that bottle to this day.

One last crucial observation: With each stall we entered, with each shop we went into, Carmelita's connection with the owners was always personal. It was about relationships. Carmelita knew these people well, and they knew her. They were *amici* (friends).

This wasn't a mega grocery store with an impersonal transaction of a pre-packaged product. Each shop owner took the time to talk to Carmelita and us. They were exceptionally proud to show us their products and discuss their origins. Only after that was finished to their satisfaction was the business at hand taken care of. Such a gentle way of life.

Once our purchases were complete, we walked to Carmelita's apartment. It was a charming walk, and along the way, she pointed to a nondescript building and invited us to follow her. We followed her across the street and walked up to the second floor, where we were amazed to discover women, most of whom were *nonnas* (grandmothers), making fresh tortellini. It was an impressive operation and an experience quite unlike any other we have had.

Seeing all that fresh pasta reminded me how hungry I was. At Carmelita's apartment, we then baked, cooked, made homemade pasta quills, and sipped wine before sitting down to our gastronomic delight.

SEASON IV
A Cremonese Legacy Secured

———

Buying a Cremonese Marvel

———

CHERI AND I were now filled with a sense of determination and mission. We were going to try to buy the Ceruti. We both strongly felt that out of respect for Mr. Phillips, our first step should be to write to him and explain that we were seriously considering approaching the Louisville Orchestra with an offer to purchase it. We treasured—coveted, actually—his input and wanted to know if, in his opinion, our making such an offer would in any way appear disrespectful to Mr. Will's legacy. We wanted Mr. Phillips' blessing.

We were ecstatic when his response arrived. He enthusiastically encouraged our quest. In response to our letter, he sent a detailed, three-page reply.

His reply reminded me of reading the ending of a Hercule Poirot novel. Poirot always calls the characters and suspects together and slowly, methodically explains not only who committed the murder, but how. By the time he is finished, all becomes clear, and the pieces have fallen into place.

Through Mr. Phillips' reply, all the pieces fell into place, and everything became clear. He wrote:

> Bill Hedden and I together decided that your playing the Ceruti in the Louisville Orchestra would be the means of sharing it with thousands of listeners over a period of many years. Since you were not a 501c (3) as defined in the Internal Revenue Code and the Louisville Orchestra was, the Louisville Orchestra would be the recipient of the violin with the provision that you

would be the player and custodian of it as long as you
were a member of the orchestra.

Over these three marvelous pages, he gave us a wonderful
summary, reviewing the history of the violin leading up to Mr.
Will's decision to gift it to the orchestra. He concluded by giving
us his blessing to purchase the Ceruti. In fact, should it be necessary, he encouraged us to offer his letter if the orchestra needed
more information.

With yet another hurdle out of the way, it was time to approach the orchestra's executive director with our offer. One thing
we knew for certain, we never wanted to be put in this position
again. We had come much too close to losing Cheri's voice—this
magnificent instrument, this Cremonese marvel.

But we still had to contend with the issue of cost, the stickiest
part of this transaction. What was a fair price? Our solution was
straightforward. Cheri and I proposed that we write the orchestra
a check for the exact amount for which the violin was insured. We
were relieved when there was no disagreement on their part. In
fact, they enthusiastically agreed.

I readily admit that for us the purchase price was steep—six
figures steep. It took me some time to come to peace with the
amount of our offer, an amount that, at least around our house, is
a lot of money. But then I remembered something Oscar Wilde
had said: "Nowadays, people know the price of everything and the
value of nothing." That quote resonated deep within my soul. Having come so close to losing the Ceruti, I embraced the value and
privilege of owning such an instrument. I was completely at peace
with our decision at last.

I was also thankful to be in the financial position to be able
purchase it. No financing, no loans, just an all-cash transaction. I
was becoming increasingly excited to think through and appreciate
what a privilege it would be to own such an instrument.

The day of our meeting finally arrived. As you would expect, we were nervous, given what was at stake. But it couldn't have gone any smoother, and the rest, as they say, is history. The Ceruti was finally ours!

The Treasure Trove, a.k.a. the Hall of the Greats

IN THE BEAUTIFUL historic center of Cremona stands the impressive Museo del Violino. I tend to think of it more as a monument, a cathedral actually, created to venerate the Cremonese family dynasties that have given us the greatest violins ever made. This certainly isn't just another stuffy old museum. It's a technological wonder that opened to the public in September 2013.

We were visiting the *museo* on a beautiful sunny Sunday—Mother's Day, 2017. We were impressed with the way the museum uses technology to transport visitors back to the sixteenth, seventeenth, and eighteenth centuries, giving them a glimpse into a world that has long since disappeared.

The *museo* itself is comprised of ten rooms/exhibits. The moment you begin your tour, you are immersed in the world of the violin. It reminded me of a person studying a foreign language who decides to take an immersion course. During their study, one language and one language only is spoken, and it isn't their native tongue. Inside the world of this *museo,* that language is violin.

One exhibit provided a sense and scents of what a violin maker's workshop of the Golden Age must have looked and smelled like. After all, wood and varnish have very distinctive aromas.

Another exhibit allowed us to experience the exquisite, pure sound of a Stradivari violin through an acoustic high-tech dome with twenty-four loudspeakers placed at the center of the room.

As we continued our tour, I felt a reaction welling up inside me that I didn't expect, a reaction that tugged at my senses and emotions—a visceral response.

An Italian phrase kept running through my mind: *"Tutto fatto a mano."* Literally translated, it means, "All made by hand."

The irony of that moment and that phrase was not lost on me. Here we were, surrounded by all this marvelous technology. Yet, these instruments were *"tutto fatto a mano!"* None of this technology was available to these craftsmen. Stradivari didn't even use sandpaper. Think of that! But such is the touch of a genius. I still marvel at this.

Enigmatically, the *museo* has brilliantly managed to leverage technology to bring these two seemingly incompatible worlds together. It entices the visitor to enter into a more intimate relationship with these master craftsmen—as if you were standing behind them, looking over their shoulders. Technology is used as an underpinning, always playing a supporting role to ensure that the true stars are the makers and the instruments. While it's embedded throughout the exhibits, it's never intrusive.

Pausing to take it all in, you can't help but conclude that these violins are technological wonders—acoustic machines without electronics. In this place, these two worlds of technology and fine, old, Italian violins seem to have found the perfect way to co-exist.

In my world, however, our Ceruti and technology do not always peacefully co-exist. Over the years, Cheri has never passed up the opportunity to remind me of this fact, especially when our computers or Wi-Fi aren't behaving. She will often quip, "My Ceruti is over two hundred years old, and it works twenty-four hours a day, seven days a week, without plugs, without needing to be recharged, without Wi-Fi or internet connections, or any other modern convenience." Her point is insightful and well-taken. There is not now, nor will there ever be, a Ceruti Version 2.0.

As we continued our tour, we experienced one of life's rare moments when an unexpected gift seemed to materialize out of nowhere.

We were about to have our breath taken away.

We had just finished one of the more fascinating rooms, Exhibit 6. On display are a great number of tools and gadgets that Stradivari used throughout his lengthy career. As you exit, you are left to wonder how such perfection came from such common tools.

From there, we meandered on to Exhibit 5, the room Cheri and I were most excited to see. As we entered, a plaque announced that this room was called "The Treasure Trove." Some have called it "The Treasure Box." I prefer to call it what I've heard it referred to most often, "The Hall of the Greats." Without question, that is much more appropriate.

The room is long, narrow, and dimly lit. The floors are covered in dark red carpet. The walls also seemed to be covered with a carpet-like fabric. Inconspicuous floor and ceiling lighting ran the length of the hall.

Displayed in the hall were several Cremonese instruments. All were of immense value, to be sure, but of even more historical importance. Each instrument was shown in its own case, like privileged prima donnas on display. The pedestal upon which the display case rested was about four feet tall. It consisted of clear glass on all four sides. This configuration allowed a person 360-degree viewing.

Inside, the instrument was suspended by the scroll from the top of the case with what appeared to be two clear nylon strings. The bottom of the instrument was also secured. Individual spotlights enabled the viewer to examine every aspect, every crevice of the instrument. A plaque explained who the maker was, what the instrument was, and the year it was made. "Hall of the Greats," indeed: Amati, Stradivari, and Guarneri were among the violin makers whose instruments were displayed.

Standing this close to such perfection, I experienced that visceral reaction again. It wasn't troubling in any way—it was more a sense of awe and wonderment. I couldn't help but think that these instruments were conceived, created, and touched by these genius-es all those years ago. It was a deeply reverential moment.

We took our time wandering from display case to display case, commenting on each instrument, until we were stopped dead in our tracks in front of one violin. Surely our eyes were deceiving us. We felt the need to pinch ourselves to ensure we weren't dreaming. But there it was, a gorgeous piccolo violino, circa 1802, which is typically a violin smaller than a full-size violin and usually intend-ed to be played by younger violinists, made by none other than Giovanni Battista Ceruti!

We were ecstatic, stunned, speechless. Well, to be honest, if you knew Cheri and me, you would know the speechless part didn't last long. The similarities between this Ceruti and Cheri's were un-mistakable.

We both knew that Ceruti was a gifted and important violin maker, but honestly, we asked ourselves, what was one of his violins doing hanging in the Hall of the Greats?

We were very clearheaded about the reality that no one would ever or will ever confuse a Ceruti for a Stradivari or a Guarneri del Gesu. So, why was it here?

The answer was forthcoming, and it finally brought us full circle on the subject of the Golden Age.

The history of Cremona shows that the community of its resi-dents, certainly of these great makers, and especially Stradivari and Guarneri del Gesu, was close. They lived in close proximity.

The documentary *Violin Masters: Two Gentlemen of Cremona* includes interviews with various experts regarding Stradivari and Guarneri del Gesu. One of them, violin maker and historian Carlo Chiesa, observes, "It is obvious today that they knew each other because they lived very close to each other—next door one to the other. And Guarneri del Gesu grew up together with the last-born of Antonio's sons. They probably went to church and to school to-gether while they were in their youth."

Even the workshops of these two masters were less than a block apart.

The point is, they knew each other well. They were *amici*. Friends to the extent that when Stradivari passed away in 1737 at the age of ninety-three, Guarneri del Gesu was a pallbearer at his funeral.

However, when Guarneri del Gesu passed away in 1744 at the young age of forty-six, it seemed as if the Golden Age was at last coming to an end. Younger violin makers were no longer following the Cremonese traditions. They were striking out on their own, trying new and innovative techniques.

The very traditions that had made Cremonese violin making great were now in danger of being forgotten—violin making in Cremona was in a deep depression. But it appears that was the reason Ceruti was represented in the Hall of the Greats. The Ceruti family was destined to become the last of the great Cremonese dynasties.

In the year that Guarneri del Gesu died, 1744, and just when it seemed that the Golden Age had ended, another Cremonese maker by the name of Lorenzo Storioni came to the forefront. Storioni is the maker who is credited with revitalizing, reinvigorating, and restoring the Cremonese tradition. Fortunately, Storioni had two followers who would also carry on these revered Cremonese violin-making traditions, one of whom was Giovanni Battista Ceruti.

Following Storioni's death in 1816, the Ceruti family rose to prominence and dominated this violin renaissance of sorts for three generations. Giovanni Battista Ceruti, his son Giuseppe, and grandson Enrico comprised the Ceruti dynasty that eventually died out, ultimately bringing the Golden Age to an end.

Upon reflection, and in an effort to understand the important role Ceruti played, I find it helpful to think of bookends. I have not uncovered any authoritative source that would describe it this way, but it creates a mental image I find useful.

Andrea Amati and his dynasty were the first bookend that ushered in the Golden Age. Giovanni Battista Ceruti and his dynasty were the second bookend that ushered it out. This must surely be why the Ceruti was proudly displayed in the Hall of the Greats.

The legacy of our Ceruti was now evident to us. While the quality of Ceruti's instruments will never equal the quality of a Stradivari or Guarneri del Gesu, his place in Cremonese violin-making history is nonetheless secure. His skills and contributions earned him the privilege of being counted among the most important of the Cremonese makers.

Interestingly, one of the museum's docents standing nearby noticed our excitement over this particular violin. In fact, she got very excited herself once we informed her that Cheri owned a G.B. Ceruti, circa 1810. She was a lovely and gracious woman and a great ambassador for the *museo*.

As we chatted, she asked us if we would be willing to loan our Ceruti to the *museo* to be displayed in the Hall of the Greats. We were flabbergasted and flattered at the same time. But the answer was a resounding no, for the simple reason that for Cheri, this violin is a tool of her trade. They are meant to be and need to be played, and Cheri plays the Ceruti virtually every day.

At some point, old age will overtake us with all its aches and pains, which, by the way, makes playing the violin even more difficult than it already is. And at that moment, Cheri and I will pass out of the Ceruti's life, and a new gifted, deserving violinist will enter. But after having had this experience, we are comforted knowing that while we will be forgotten, Giovanni Battista Ceruti's legacy will continue.

An important digression is needed here. Why are institutions such as the Museo del Violino so critically needed? There are many reasons, but one of the most interesting is that these fine instruments are made of wood, and that means they are highly temperamental—they are especially susceptible to changes in temperature and humidity. To eliminate this danger to the greatest extent possible, Cheri's violin case, for example—like so many—has a built-in humidifier, thermometer, and hygrometer to keep the Ceruti's environment within the case as stable as possible.

But the harsh reality is Cheri still must use it daily. It simply doesn't matter whether it's a bitterly cold day in January or a brutally hot, hazy, humid day in August. Just like her, it has to go to work.

All these factors can profoundly affect the instrument. Just the fact they are hundreds of years old and yet are subject to the schedules of current-day soloists jet-setting around the world puts them at risk of being damaged through normal wear and tear.

Cheri's Ceruti constantly reminds us of the upkeep and maintenance these instruments demand. In the worst-case scenario, a restoration will be required if damage occurs to the violin. This isn't an overly concerning issue in the hands of a gifted restorer. Every effort will be made to remove or replace as little of the original varnish or wood as possible.

But that isn't always what happens. Restoration repairs can be sloppy or poorly done. Sadly, each time one of these great violins is subjected to an inferior restoration, we lose more of our ability to see how the instrument appeared in its original state.

Over dinner one evening, Philip Kass, the respected expert, appraiser, consultant, and writer who we have worked with for years, pointed out that the more extensive repairs that are required, the further away we get from seeing and holding what the maker originally created. As the years pass and new generations of repairmen and restorers are trained, they will be able to see less and less of how a Stradivari, a del Gesu, or a Ceruti, for that matter, appeared in its original state. This will diminish their ability to understand the original condition of these outstanding instruments and how to be as unobtrusive as possible when restoration or repair is required.

There are some rare exceptions, however. Philip explained how fortunate we are to have a violin made by Stradivari in 1716, famously named the Messiah.

Just as an aside, the name *the Messiah* comes from an offhand-ed remark made to the famous Italian violin collector and dealer Tarisio: "Really, Mr. Tarisio, your violin is like the Messiah of the Jews: One always expects him, but he never appears."

That sarcastic statement was referring to the fact that the Messiah was rarely played in public. It was and still is essentially a collector's piece. This is one of the very few violins we know of made by Stradivari that is in its original or "new" state. It has seldom been played. In other words, today it looks pretty much the same as it did when Stradivari handed it over to its new owner in 1716.

The Messiah is on display in the Ashmolean Museum in Oxford, England. This is a gift of incomparable importance because it shows us exactly how the instrument looked when Stradivari completed it. New generations of violin repairmen, restorers, and *luthiers* can go to the museum and see for themselves the brilliance of Stradivari's work, unscathed and untouched by time and repairs. As of 2020, the Messiah Stradivari was valued at $20 million. In reality, it is priceless.

How do you celebrate such a glorious day in Cremona and try to absorb all that has happened? With food and wine, of course. We found a charming outdoor restaurant and relived our unforget-table day, while savoring a lunch of homemade pumpkin-stuffed ravioli and delicious grilled fish. This naturally was accompanied by a sampling of Cremona's local wines.

Following our lunch, we walked around the city and discov-ered it is still very much the violin-making capital. The streets are lined with shop after shop of contemporary *luthiers*. Many, in fact, will argue that the new violin makers in Cremona have elevated the art form to a new Golden Age. Time and history will be the final arbiter of that claim.

Philip Kass

———

THE POET BRIAN A. "Drew" Chalker wrote, "People come into your life for a reason, a season, or a lifetime." Cheri and I are so grateful that Philip Kass entered our life for both a reason and a lifetime.

Both Cheri's and my relationship with Moennig & Son began in 1972. After Mr. Moennig III passed away in 2004, we were fortunate to continue our relationship with the firm. Our primary contact became Philip Kass, a Moennig associate who spent twenty-five years at Moennig & Son.

Philip Kass
Photo by Christopher Germain

Philip is a gifted and fascinating individual. He has many talents, including being an appraiser, consultant, lecturer, and writer on fine classic stringed instruments and bows. Cheri and I have known him now for almost fifty years. It is always a privilege to spend time with him.

From 1977 until 2002, in his role at Moennig's, Philip held and examined many of the world's greatest violins. His expertise, training, and hands-on experience came from studying with William Moennig III, William Moennig Jr., and the great Italian violin maker and appraiser Dario D'Attili. He supplemented his studies with independent travel, inquiries, and research. He is now one of the industry's most respected and sought-after authorities on fine, rare, stringed instruments and bows, Italian and otherwise.

Violinists must regularly get their instruments appraised to be sure the appraised value stays within proximity of the insured value. Reappraisals are essential, due to the way these instruments appreciate. Philip is the expert who has performed these periodic appraisals of the Ceruti. Appraisals are typically done every two to three years.

In the 1990s, Philip also came to some new conclusions about our Ceruti. You recall that Bill Moennig III had initially identified it as having been "born" in 1780. However, in the 1990s, Philip was involved in some research being done in Cremona. What the researchers determined was that since Ceruti was forty years old before he began his career as a violin maker, it was highly unlikely that our Ceruti could have been made prior to 1800. Thus the date of 1780 could be ruled out.

As the years passed and as Philip examined more Cerutis and the dates they were made—factoring in such things as the quality of the wood used—he was comfortably able to say our Ceruti was most likely made somewhere between 1805 and 1810, ultimately attributing the date to 1810.

The reappraisal ritual we have had with Philip is always a highlight for Cheri and me. Typically, we fly to Philadelphia to meet with him. His knowledge and expertise are encyclopedic. I've often wondered if the man has a photographic memory, due to the sheer amount of knowledge he is able to conjure up.

Since he lives outside of Philadelphia, he takes the train into the city and meets us at our hotel. I might add, the hotel we usually stay at is—you guessed it: 1715 at Rittenhouse, a Boutique Hotel, just across from Rittenhouse Square, inside the Rittenhouse District. Kudzu!

Not content to rely solely on an appraiser's memory, the company that insures the Ceruti requires that Philip provide a visual appraisal from time to time. This means he must physically inspect the instrument to determine its condition and value. And so we often invite him to our suite, where he carefully performs the visual appraisal. He follows that up in a few days with a letter stating his findings, including the new valuation. We, in turn, forward this information to the insurance company. Mission accomplished.

When the task of reappraising the violin is behind us, we are free to sit back, relax, and share a bottle of wine while discussing the latest news from the Louisville Orchestra. As friends are prone to do, this naturally includes swapping news from other orchestras around the country. Without a doubt, however, the most fascinating portion of our time together is hearing about the travels he has undertaken since our last visit. My observation is that Philip is a modest man who would never boast about his accomplishments. But in the ordinary discourse between us, he shares the most interesting experiences.

One visit in 2017 perfectly illustrates the extent to which this man will travel for the sake of research and his profession.

Earlier that year, Cheri and I had made our annual visit to Italy, specifically to the Piedmont region. We had two objectives during this trip. First, to enjoy the Barolo and Barbaresco wines the region is famous for, and second, to take the opportunity to spend that wonderful day in Cremona.

While in the Piedmont region, we stayed in a stunning renovated medieval castle, Castello di Sinio. Our host was the wonderful restorer, owner, manager, and chef of the Castello, Denise Pardini. Her knowledge of the region's wine is equally impressive. She recommended that Cheri and I take a four-hour course about Barolo and Barbaresco wines, which we did. We walked away with an entirely new appreciation for these lovely wines, although we had been enjoying them for years.

The Castello was originally built in 1142 and is located in the tiny medieval village of Sinio. This is a small, small hamlet. Did I mention it is small? So you can imagine our surprise when Philip informed us that he, too, had visited Sinio. But he went neither in the capacity of a tourist nor to put his feet up while drinking wine and relaxing at the Castello.

Not at all. Philip was there to speak to the priest of Sinio's parish church. His purpose, as I recall, was to attempt to authenticate whether the wife of another famous Italian violin maker, Giovanni Pressenda, was originally from Sinio.

While Philip would never admit it, his Italian must be well advanced, if not fluent. He mentioned, in passing, that the parish priest spoke no English. Such is Philip Kass.

As our conversation continues and the Philadelphia afternoon fades into evening, we move to one of Philadelphia's excellent Italian restaurants. Long evenings including marvelous dinners, magnificent conversation, and, of course, outstanding wine.

Over the years, we've shared several wonderful meals and wonderful wines, but none are as rich or meaningful as our conversations and friendship.

A Word About Rare Italian Violins as Investments

———

THIS IS A subject of endless fascination. As I have described our journey, I have alluded to Cheri's Ceruti not only in terms of its qualities as a fine, old, Italian violin but also as an investment. As it turns out, purchasing the Ceruti has been the single best investment decision we've made during my forty-year career. All these years later, I now also grasp and appreciate that fine, old, Italian violins, much like rare paintings, are the ultimate in alternative investments They appreciate in ways more ordinary investments never will.

For a long time, I had known that fine, old, Italian instruments had the potential to be superb investments. These instruments don't react to market influences in the same way or to the same degree as more typical investments. This also means that the "ride" you experience over the long term is smoother and less dramatic.

Violins like Cheri's fall into an asset class of their own known as "alternative investments." You are probably familiar with more traditional alternative investments such as precious metals (think gold and silver), real estate (both commercial and residential), and such commodities as pork bellies.

The reality is, however, fine, old, Italian instruments make wonderful alternative investments because, as I mentioned earlier, they don't behave or react to external or internal market forces in the same way more traditional alternative investments do, with sudden drops or increases that can make for a stressful rollercoaster ride.

The demand for fine, old, Italian instruments began seriously taking off in the 1960s for several reasons. One of the most obvious was Economics 101: supply and demand. The demand for these instruments was exploding as more and more buyers flooded the market—not just from Europe and the United States, but expanding to Russia, Japan, and China as well.

However, as the demand increased, the limited supply remained the same for one very obvious reason: Stradivari, Guarneri, and Ceruti were all dead and weren't making any new instruments. That, perhaps, is the ultimate supply chain problem.

When it comes to investing in fine, old, Italian violins, the top investment tiers need to be carefully considered and studied.

I like to think of the top investment tier violins (Strads and Guarneri del Gesu's) as being Rolls-Royces and Bentleys, or even a Bugatti. A Ceruti would fall into a lesser investment tier, which I would compare to a Mercedes Benz or a BMW. While perhaps not the quality of a Rolls-Royce or Bentley, Mercedes and BMWs are still superb automobiles.

Perhaps now you will also begin to understand and appreciate that just as no one will ever confuse a Mercedes Benz or a BMW for a Rolls-Royce or a Bentley, likewise, in the world of fine, old, Italian violins, no one will ever confuse a Ceruti for a Strad or a Guarneri del Gesu.

It should come as no surprise then that the top investment tier consists of two makers and two makers only: Antonio Stradivari and Guarneri del Gesu. These two makers represent the best that fine, old, Italian violins have to offer. Thus their prices tend to increase year after year, as do their rates of return. However, even here, one must be careful. Violins made during Stradivari's "golden years" are amongst his finest and will deliver investment performance far above earlier Strads.

In today's market, prices for these instruments are consistently in the $5 million to $20 million range. According to a study quoted in the *Economist*, the annual rate of return for a Stradivari violin between 1980 and 2011 was an extraordinary 15.4 percent. That is remarkable!

The next investment tier consists of violins made by makers such as Giovanni Battista Guadagnini. These instruments are neither as pricey as Strads or Guarneri del Gesu's and neither are their rates of return as rich. For example, depending on the condition, a Guadagnini can be bought for anywhere from $500,000 to over $2 million.

Next comes the investment tier made up of makers such as Ceruti. At the time of this writing, a Ceruti violin in excellent condition would not exceed $500,000. The annual rate of return Cheri and I have experienced from 2000 until 2023 is 6.5 percent, which is very much in line with similar fine, old, Italian violins in the same investment tier.

It turns out that the finer instrument you can afford to buy, especially one with a colorful history, the higher your expected annual rate of return should be.

But as the demand and the prices continue to explode, the issue once again becomes that the very musicians these instruments were made for are being priced out, with most violins well beyond their financial grasp.

When this is the case, what happens next is often one of two scenarios. First, the musician will settle for an instrument by the same maker but of lesser quality and prestige. Or, secondly, they will forgo the maker in favor of another maker whose instruments are of less quality and value but more affordable. Obviously, either of these scenarios means less expectation of both growth potential and rate of return.

Keeping all that information in mind, we feel so grateful and blessed to own this instrument. But our feelings of blessing and gratefulness have been magnified ten-fold over the years by the many people who have come into our lives as a result of owning this Cremonese marvel.

Season IV Author's Whim:
Villa Poggiano, Our Italian Famiglia

———

Legacies come in many forms. Clearly, Season IV and the Museo del Violino have been a testament to the legacy of Giovanni Battista Ceruti. But legacies also come in the form of friendships and relationships. Such is the case with our dear friend Stefania Savini and our beloved Villa Poggiano.

Famiglia (family), *amici* (friends), *bucolica* (bucolic), and *paradiso* (heaven): When I dream of Tuscany and specifically Villa Poggiano, these are the words that come to mind. Just thinking of time spent at the Villa transports me to a place of tranquility and calm.

Villa Poggiano is nestled in the beautiful Tuscan hillside, just three kilometers outside the historic town of Montepulciano. This medieval town has a rich history and is known for many things, but none more than its famous wine, Vino Nobile di Montepulciano.

Villa Poggiano is a short drive beyond the town, just past the historically significant Church of San Biagio situated on your right. No more than a kilometer further down the road, turn left onto an off-the-beaten-track, paved road, and you will meander your way up to the Villa's iron gates.

If you close your eyes and dream of Tuscany and its villas, Villa Poggiano is everything you would imagine a Tuscan villa should be. The beautiful gates open to invite you to enter. The gravel drive is lined with tall, majestic Cypress trees. Sitting at the end of this drive is a large orcio terracotta urn, which is always filled with colorful flowers—just another way the Villa's owner, Stefania, and the

Villa itself say, "Welcome, friends. You are entering a special place."

With each visit, as we approach the iron gates, a sense of calm begins to envelop us. Cheri and I look at each other and realize that this adopted Italian home of ours is gorgeous, but the best is still to come: At the end of the drive, our dear friend Stefania is waiting with open arms and big hugs,

Stefania is beautiful, charismatic, energetic, and a charming host. Her keen eye for detail and her contagious laugh make you fall in love with her and the Villa straightaway.

Her passion is evident, serving her guests and putting their needs above everything else. When I pass by the reception desk, I typically find Stefania huddled with a couple, a family, or a group, helping them plan their day. She is the mastermind, the talent, and the visionary that makes Villa Poggiano the enchanting place it is.

Cheri (right) with our dear friend Stefania

As each of our visits comes to a close, Cheri and I offer a prayer, "Thank you, Lord, for this place and for allowing us to be part of it. And please bring us back next year!"

Italians speak with great respect and reverence about the rhythm of time: the rhythm of each day, each season, each year, and ultimately the rhythm of life. As a musician, Cheri is keenly attuned to rhythm, too—but not just musical rhythm. We slip effortlessly into the time-honored rhythms and patterns of the day at the Villa and in Tuscany. They suit us perfectly.

Stefania summarizes it best: "Villa Poggiano is not a hotel, but a home we wish to share with guests to our beautiful Montepulciano area, where life is simple, the silence magical, and the daily pattern of one's days follows the time-honored rhythms of nature."Time spent at the Villa puts us in a perfectly peaceful state of mind. We feel safe; we feel content, with no cares to distract us.

So it is at Villa Poggiano. A taste of heaven on earth to be sure! There's no place we'd rather be.

One Final Whim: Lunch and a Life Lesson

W E WERE ON a day-long Brunello tasting and tour near Montalcino. It was time for *pranzo* (lunch).

As we turned off the narrow road and onto the gravel driveway, our tour guide, Rebecca, turned to our group and said, "Alberto and his wife, Marzia, are simple farmers who are in their seventies who also make exceptional olive oil. They produce a thousand bottles each year. They don't speak a word of English, they wouldn't know what to do with a credit card if they had one, and during their lifetime, neither one of them has traveled more than thirty-five kilometers (about twenty-four miles) away from where we're standing. But they are wonderful people, and I've been bringing my wine tour groups to them for years now."

And with that, we were introduced to Alberto and Marzia. We all exchanged smiles and made awkward attempts to say, "*Piacere*" ("It's a pleasure to meet you"), in an effort to break the ice. It was one of those times when although we felt a bit self-conscious, we just kept smiling and nodding. Surely that must be a universal gesture: Smile and nod, smile and nod.

As the sunlight shone through the vines, Alberto enthusiastically motioned for us to follow him down a terraced, gravel path. We were escorted to a long, beautifully set wooden table under an equally long trellis covered with vines. Two rustic lanterns hung above the table, indicating that dining alfresco in the evening was a ritual. The sun was at full strength, the sky was a deep, beautiful blue. It was a glorious Tuscan day.

Yet, this experience, this *pranzo*, these two simple farmers, were about to remind Cheri and me of one of life's most important lessons. Contentment, fulfillment, satisfaction, joy—these are the words that came to mind as I watched Alberto and Marzia going about their work, serving us a truly memorable meal.

Notice, I did not use the word *happy* to describe them. Being happy and being joyful are two different states of being. While being joyful is lasting, happiness can be fleeting.

The two of them were joyful. The smiles on their faces welled up from deep within. These smiles were genuine, smiles that showed they took delight in their work of serving others.

Marzia was our Tuscan *capocuoca* (chef), and Alberto, wearing a simple white T-shirt and a white apron, served the meal. As each course was served, they could both hear the elated commentary coming from all of us. The food was delicious, and the experience was very special.

Marzia and Alberto clearly understood what it meant to be content with their lives—lives many might consider tedious. They were very particular about everything they did, including the organic farming methods they incorporated in their agronomy. Even their olive oil is pressed using the traditional method of crushing the olives with two enormous stone wheels.

As for the meal, our *antipasti* (first) course consisted of traditional crostini, tomatoes, zucchini, and bread, served with exceptional olive oil. The *primi piatti* (second) course was a homemade Tagliatelle with meat sauce. The *secondi piatti* (third) course consisted of slightly breaded flattened chicken, fried and served with roasted red peppers, onion, and thinly sliced potatoes in a "secret sauce." Throughout this feast, Alberto made certain that the Chianti produced by his neighbor flowed freely.

For *dolce* (dessert), Alberto simply picked up a basket and a pair of shears, reached above him into the grape vines, harvested several clusters of white grapes, and rinsed them off. They were sweet and so delicious.

Seeing the joy in Alberto and Marzia as they prepared and served our *pranzo* reminded Cheri and me of the importance of being content with what you have in life. I felt a bond with the two of our hosts, although we were never able to speak to each other. They reminded us of the importance of this life lesson, without ever having said a word.

Alberto and Marzia

EPILOGUE

———

I'M SITTING IN my office on a bright September morning—
one of those glorious mornings when all seems right with the
world. As I gaze out my windows, enjoying the vibrant green leaves
set against an amazing azure sky, the expression once again runs
through my mind, "You never truly own one of these great violins.
You simply pass through its life."

The passing of time and the inevitable aging process accom-
panying it are constant reminders of this truth and our mortality.
And as if we need to be reminded, with the loss of each family
member, friend, or loved one, we become more painfully aware of
our own impermanence.

Prior to the deaths of all four of our parents, we watched them
age through their sixties, seventies, and eighties, and in the case of
my mom, into her nineties. As the losses of our family and their
friends mounted, we also saw the toll it took on them.

Upon receiving news of the passing of another relative or
friend, my dad would sit in his favorite wingback recliner, resting
his head against the back of the chair. And while pensively staring
at the ceiling, he would say with great melancholy in his voice,
"We come, and we go." He could be a man of few words when he
chose, but there was an infinite amount of love for those who had
passed, as well as sadness and deep loss, behind those five simple
words.

Such a painful reminder visited our home in January 2022.
We received word that at the age of ninety-four, my mentor and

our dear friend, Mr. Phillips, had passed away at his home in New Orleans. The reality of that loss sent me reeling. I still feel the deep pain and void of his passing.

But as is often the case, his death proved to be the catalyst, the push I needed, finally convincing me of the importance of writing this book. The story of this extraordinary journey needed to be told, and telling it has been a cathartic experience.

As you might also expect, as time has marched relentlessly forward, most of the people who played key roles in our journey have also passed. They were all wonderful, important people, and I felt strongly that the stories of the roles they so generously played also deserved to be told.

We, too, have entered a new season of life. While Cheri will never retire from playing the violin, she did retire from her full-time chair with the Louisville Orchestra, opting instead to play part-time.

Rest assured, however, that the Ceruti is far from retired—quite the opposite, in fact. Cheri continues to practice and play daily, putting the violin through her demanding rigors. I will say she and the Ceruti are working as hard as ever. They have never sounded better!

As she plays it, coaxing it to its full potential, you can sense the Ceruti filling its sonorous lungs, placing all its marvelous capabilities at her disposal. Those quintessentially Italian characteristics—the arched wood plates, and its soul fully resonating, flooding the air with that exquisite sound and glorious music. They're both at the top of their game.

Cheri's passion for sharing the journey of the violin and the Heddens also lives on. She is still occasionally asked to speak to groups recounting the Ceruti's journey. She is honored because in doing so, she keeps alive the memory of the people who made our dream a reality. But most importantly, she honors Mr. Will.

I never tire of sitting in my office each day, listening to the music emanating from Cheri's studio. Today it's Bach, Ysaye, and Mozart. It's a good day.

As my appreciation and love for these great Cremonese instruments grows, so does my sense of respect and awe for them. I have renewed admiration for the immeasurable contributions they have made to our culture, our society, and our civilization. In light of our ownership of such a fine, rare instrument, I am of the humble opinion that the fame, the romance, the importance, and the charisma of the Golden Age and these great Cremonese makers will live on well into the future.

But as for today, the here and now, I can think of no more fitting tribute to end this season of our journey than to quote an homage paid to the two giants of Cremonese violin making, Stradivari and Guarneri del Gesu. In the moving documentary entitled *Violin Masters: Two Gentlemen of Cremona*, narrator Alfred Molina closes the documentary with this tribute:

> Somewhere tonight, in one of the world's great concert halls, a violin will take the stage, whose soaring voice, elegant craft, and deep sense of tradition, will connect it through three centuries to Piazza San Domenico, to Antonio Stradivari and Guarneri del Gesu—the two gentlemen of Cremona, the greatest violin makers the world has ever known.

And with that, our journey with the Ceruti—our Ceruti—has come full circle. It is humbling to know that this violin, this seemingly lighter-than-air marvel, can be traced back to the very same Piazza San Domenico in Cremona and that very same Cremonese heritage and tradition.

As it has done for over two hundred years, the Ceruti will continue to do what it was created to do: delight, thrill, and comfort souls. And whoever has the privilege of passing through its life in the years to come will undoubtedly find the immense pleasure in it that Cheri has.

In the meantime, though, our Ceruti will continue to provide immeasurable gratification and fulfillment for the two of us.

ACKNOWLEDGEMENTS

As I began this project, I was concerned whether our journey of acquiring the Ceruti would make a sufficiently interesting story to hold the reader's attention. I felt it needed something more. That is why I decided to intermingle several Italian travel experiences Cheri and I have savored over the years.

However, as is often the case, I got a bit carried away—in fact, to the extent that the "travelogue" was taking away from the story of our violin's journey. I couldn't see that at first. But then along came a superb editor named Jill Johnson Keeney, who was as much a blessing as she was direct and honest with me. She gently persuaded me that much of what I had thought was entertaining dialogue was actually distracting, extraneous material that needed to go. Jill's patience and her willingness to school me in these matters is how my book reached its final conclusion, and I am so proud of the finished product. Her comments, criticism, and suggestions (sometimes insistent suggestions) have made this a better book—a far better book.

Getting to know Jill has been a privilege and a joy. Words are not adequate to convey the depth of my gratefulness for her help and guidance.

Once I mustered the courage to allow an editor to read my manuscript and became interested to see if it had "legs," I recalled Jill had said John Clark of Old Stone Press was publishing David Jones' book, *Always Moving Forward*. On a whim, I contacted John to see if he might be interested in my manuscript.

John could not have been more enthusiastic or encouraging as he undertook this endeavor. Throughout the process, he sent uplifting and supportive emails. Again, I could not be happier or more proud of the finished product and the care and skillful detail John has lavished on this book.

I am immensely gratified that both John and Jill are now an integral part of our journey and the journey of this marvelous Cremonese violin.

ABOUT THE AUTHOR

TOM KELLEY IS a retired businessman and appreciates all things Italian: food, wine, art, opera, orchestral music, and the Italian people. He is married to Cheri Lyon Kelley, a semi-retired violinist with the Louisville Orchestra. She and her remarkable violin have performed for audiences both at home and abroad for more than forty-five years. Tom enjoys nothing more than spending a quiet evening at home with Cheri and their son, Ethan.

Breakfast in Tuscany: Tom and Cheri at Villa Poggiano during their journey to authenticate Cheri's violin.

Printed in the USA
CPSIA information can be obtained
at www.ICGtesting.com
LVHW070808131124
796421LV00006B/101